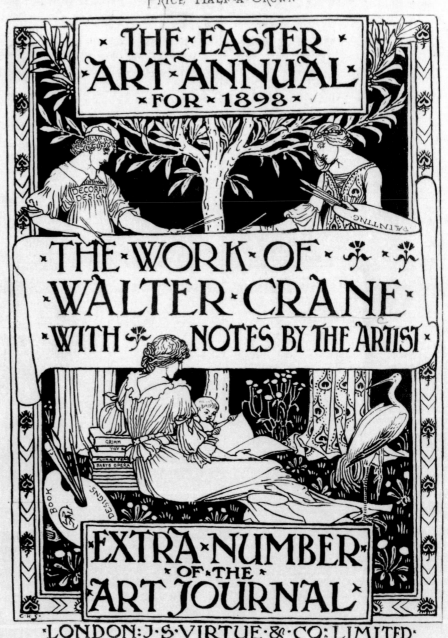

Price Half-a-Crown

THE EASTER ART ANNUAL FOR 1898

THE WORK OF WALTER CRANE

WITH NOTES BY THE ARTIST

DECORATIVE DESIGN

PAINTING

GRIMM
TOY B
FLORA'S FES
BABY'S OPERA

BOOK

DESIGNS

EXTRA NUMBER OF THE ART JOURNAL

LONDON: J·S·VIRTUE & CO: LIMITED

Edited by Greg Smith and Sarah Hyde

Walter Crane 1845-1915

Artist, Designer and Socialist

Lund Humphries · London
in association with
The Whitworth Art Gallery, University of Manchester

Frontispiece: Walter Crane *Page* from '*The Art Journal*' 1898, re-worked by Charles Hazelwood Shannon, wood-engraving

A collection of essays, with a catalogue of works
exhibited at the Whitworth Art Gallery, University of Manchester
20 January – 18 March 1989

Copyright © 1989 Whitworth Art Gallery
University of Manchester

First edition 1989
Published by
Lund Humphries Publishers Ltd
16 Pembridge Road London W11 3HL

British Library Cataloguing in Publication Data

Walter Crane, 1845–1915: artist, designer and socialist.
1. English visual arts. Crane, Walter, 1845–1915
Catalogues, indexes
I. Smith, Greg   II. Hyde, Sarah   III. Whitworth Art Gallery
709′.2′4

ISBN 0 85331 553 1

Designed by Alan Bartram
Made and printed in Great Britain by
BAS Printers Limited, Over Wallop, Hampshire

Contents

Colour plates following p68

Director's Foreword

The exhibition, so splendidly organised by Greg Smith, opens the centenary year celebrations of the Whitworth Art Gallery. The choice of Walter Crane with which to commence the year was an inspired one, for here was an artist/designer who cut across the full range of the Whitworth's collections, a man who was involved with the Manchester Art School in the early days of the fledgling Whitworth Institute, and an artist who calls for the sort of popular, but sound, scholarly treatment that has gained the Whitworth an international reputation for its exhibitions.

In realising our aim of producing a worthy successor to the *William Morris and the Middle Ages* exhibition, we have, as always, drawn upon the support of colleagues in galleries and libraries throughout the country though it is sad that we were not able to afford the foreign loans which would have enabled us to complete what, with a very few exceptions, is a remarkably complete picture of Crane's work. The fact that we came so close to our aim of comprehensiveness is not a little due to the extraordinarily generous support extended to the project by the artist's grandson, Anthony Crane, from its inception. To him and to all the other lenders, public and private, who are listed elsewhere, may I extend my grateful thanks. We are also indebted to Arthur Sanderson & Sons Ltd for providing photographic facilities at their wallpaper mill in Lancashire, and to both Sanderson's and The Fine Art Society for their generous sponsorship which has contributed to the production of this fine catalogue.

The editors would also like to thank the authors of the essays for their contributions: Joanna Banham of Arthur Sanderson & Sons Ltd; Dr Joany Hichberger of Manchester Polytechnic; Dr Jennifer Harris, Assistant Keeper, Textiles and Christine Woods, Research Assistant, Wallpapers of the Whitworth Art Gallery.

Professor C R Dodwell

Acknowledgements

This catalogue would not have been possible in its current form were it not for Isobel Spencer's excellent general account of Crane. Her thoroughness has allowed us to concentrate on a number of themes which particularly interested us and which we feel help to give a broader understanding of Crane's work. These include an analysis of Crane's writings and their meanings in relation to his work, and a detailed discussion of his working methods and his relationships with the craftsmen and manufacturers with whom he collaborated.

Putting together a comprehensive exhibition of one of the most productive artists of any time has had its problems. When, after four months' research we came across a book titled 10 *Thousand Cranes* our hearts sank; the largest collection of Crane's work and we didn't know about it. Fortunately it turned out to be an account of Japanese art! We would like to thank the following for showing us what seems at least ten thousand Cranes and for allowing us to borrow 400 or so: Michael Arnold; D B Pullen, Art Workers' Guild; Jon Whiteley, Ashmolean Museum; the staff of the Beinecke Library, Yale; Jane Farrington and Stephen Wildman, Birmingham Museum and Art Gallery; Julia Wilson, Bodleian Library, Oxford; Anthony Griffiths, Janice Reading and the staff of the Print Room, British Museum; Chris Rawlings, Media Services, British Library; John Christian; Jeremy Rex-Parkes, Christie's; Richard Dennis; Craig Hartley, Professor Michael Jaffé and David Scrase, Fitzwilliam Museum, Cambridge; Margaret Kelly and Caroline L Reitz, The FORBES Magazine Collection, New York; Albert Gallichan; Peter Rose; Hugh Stevenson, Glasgow Art Gallery and Museum; John Gorman; Liz Hall; Julian Hartnoll; Nancy Finlay, Houghton Library, Harvard; B Curle, Kensington Public Library; Alex Robertson, Anthony Wells-Cole, Leeds City Art Galleries; Messrs Rodgers, Hogan and Carrick, Liverpool City Libraries; Maurice Davis, Richard Gray, Ruth Shrigley and Julian Treuherz, Manchester City Art Galleries; Gaye Smith, Ian Rogerson and the staff of Manchester Polytechnic Library; Rachel Moss; Richard Dean, National Trust; Christopher and Jenny Newall; Mr Pratt; Pamela Adamson-Jones, Joanna Banham, Andrew Campbell, Bill Catlow, Norman Gibbon, Catherine Miller, Michael Parry, A Sanderson & Sons Ltd; Sarah Colegrave, Sotheby's; Sir Alan Bowness and Stephen Dunn, Tate Gallery; Martyn Anglesea and E V Hickey, Ulster Museum; Stephen Astley, David Coachworth, Santina Levey, J W G Mallet, John Murdoch, Linda Parry, Gill Saunders, Clive Wainwright and Eva White, Victoria and Albert Museum; Alex Kidson and Edward Morris, Walker Art Gallery, Liverpool; Lynn Miller, The Wedgwood Museum; Peter Cormack and Norah Gillow, William Morris Gallery; Colin Wilson, Susan P Casteras, Yale Center for British Art, New Haven.

May we also thank the following who, rather closer to home, have worked so hard on this project: Bob Davenport, Tony Jones, Cliff Lomax, Sue Mortimer, Ann Sumner, Joanna Taylor, Julian Tomlin, John West, Gwilym Williams, Eve Winson and all the attendant staff, plus Peter Burton and Michael Pollard for photography and Clio Jones and Ann Tullo for conservation, and a special thank you to Danielle Benn for help with research.

Finally, we would like to acknowledge the support of the University of Manchester in providing funds for extensive travel in this country and abroad.

Abbreviations

A & C:
Arts and Crafts Exhibition Society

A & C *Catalogue*:
Arts and Crafts Exhibition *Catalogue*

Cox:
Mabel Cox, 'Arts and Crafts Workers. I—Walter Crane' *The Artist* Vol 19 1897 pp24-32

A Crane, *Yale Gazette*:
Anthony Crane, 'My Grandfather, Walter Crane' *The Yale University Library Gazette* 1957 Vol 31 no 3

Crane, *Art Journal*:
Walter Crane, 'The Work of Walter Crane with Notes by the Artist' *The Art Journal Easter Art Annual* 1898

Crane, *Bases*:
Walter Crane, *The Bases of Design* 1898

Crane, *Claims*:
Walter Crane, *The Claims of Decorative Art* 1892

Crane, *Decorative Illustration*:
Walter Crane, *Of The Decorative Illustration of Books Old and New* 1896

Crane, *Essays*:
Walter Crane and others, *Arts and Crafts Essays* 1893

Crane, *Ideals*:
Walter Crane, *Ideals in Art. Papers, theoretical, practical, critical* 1905

Crane, *Imprint*:
Walter Crane, 'Notes on my own Books for Children' *The Imprint* January-June 1913 Vol I pp81-6

Crane, *Line*:
Walter Crane, *Line and Form* 1900

Crane, *Moot Points*:
Walter Crane, Lewis F Day, *Moot Points. Friendly Disputes on Art and Industry* 1903

Crane, *Morris*:
Walter Crane, *William Morris to Whistler* 1911

Crane, *Reminiscences*:
Walter Crane, *An Artist's Reminiscences* 1907

Crane, *Wallpaper Design*:
MSS of the second in a series of 'Demonstrations in Applied Design' given at South Kensington Museum, nd (probably March 1886). Kensington Public Library F(1) 39327/28

Crane, *Westminster Budget*:
'A Word about children's books. A fireside chat with Walter Crane' *The Westminster Budget* December 1895 pp23-5

E42A 1-3:
Three volumes of press cuttings, pamphlets etc, relating to Jeffrey & Co, Victoria and Albert Museum, Dept Prints and Drawings

Exh:
Exhibited

FAS:
Fine Art Society

FAS, 1891:
Fine Art Society, *A Catalogue of a Collection of Designs by Walter Crane ... with Prefatory Notes by the Artist* 1891 p12

JDA:
The Journal of Decorative Art

Konody:
P G Konody, *The Art of Walter Crane* 1902

McLean:
Ruari McLean, *The Reminiscences of Edmund Evans, Wood-engraver and Colour-printer 1826-1905* 1967

nd:
Not dated

Spencer:
Isobel Spencer, *Walter Crane* 1975

Stephens:
F G Stephens, 'The Designs of Walter Crane' *The Portfolio* 1890 pp12-19

Studio, 1894-5:
Aymer Vallance, 'Walter Crane's Paper-Hangings' *The Studio* Vol IV 1894-5

Chronology

1845   15 August: born in Liverpool, to Thomas Crane and Marie Kearsley; childhood spent in Torquay

1857   Family moved to London

1859   Apprenticed as draughtsman on wood to W J Linton for three years

1862   First painting exhibited at the Royal Academy: *The Lady of Shalott*

1865   Began designing Toy Books for Routledge; produced 2–3 books each year until 1876

1867   Began decorating and designing ceramics for Wedgwood

1870   *Love's Altar* (D1) exhibited at Old Bond Street Gallery

1871   Met William Morris, Edward Burne-Jones and Philip Webb for first time
6 September: married Mary Frances Andrews
Toured Germany, Switzerland and Italy; settled in Rome

1873   February: daughter, Beatrice, born
May: returned to London from Italy

1874   Designed first set of nursery tiles for Maw & Co

1875   Designed first wallpaper for Jeffrey & Co
Began association with the Royal School of Art Needlework

1876   May: son, Lionel, born

1877   *The Renascence of Venus* (D4) exhibited at the first Grosvenor Gallery exhibition

1880   Began work on decorations for No 1 Holland Park

1881   31 March: death of sister, Lucy
September: family went to Rome

1883   Painted *Skeleton in Armour* panels for Library of Vinland, near Newport, Rhode Island
Spring: returned to England

1884   Art Workers' Guild formed

1885   Joined the Socialist League

1886   Joined the Fabian Society

1887   Narrowly escaped injury and arrest during mass meeting at Trafalgar Square (see B2)

1888   First exhibition held by the Arts and Crafts Exhibition Society; Crane wrote introduction to catalogue

1889   *A Diver*, watercolour, won silver medal at Paris Universal Exhibition

1890   Toured Bohemia

1891   *Renascence: A Book of Verse* published
Summer: first retrospective exhibition held at the Fine Art Society
October: family went to America, accompanying a travelling exhibition of Crane's work

1892   Toured America; returned to live at 13 Holland Street
The Claims of Decorative Art published

1893   Appointed part-time Director of Design at Manchester School of Art; resigned in 1896

1896   Touring exhibition moved to Scandinavia

1898   Appointed Principal of Royal College of Art
The Bases of Design published

1899   Designed firework display for May Day celebrations at Crystal Palace
Performed in *Beauty's Awakening*, a masque by the Art Workers' Guild at the Guildhall, London

1900   Touring exhibition visited Hungary
Line and Form published
Resigned from the Fabian Society

1903   Became full member Royal Society of Painters in Watercolours

1905   *Ideals in Art* published
Received Albert Gold Medal at Society of Arts

1907   *An Artist's Reminiscences* published

1909   Signed over rights of 27 Toy Books to John Lane & Co

1912   Painted self-portrait for Uffizi

1915   14 March: died at Horsham Cottage Hospital

George Frederick Watts *Walter Crane* 1891, oil.
National Portrait Gallery, London

Greg Smith

Developing a Public Language of Art

Although a quiet man, Walter Crane had of a flair for publicity and, conceiving himself to be a public figure, took on the responsibilities which that entailed. There was not a subject which fell outside his all-encompassing view of society and the arts. It was not just that much of his work was openly didactic; he also believed that any object designed with love and skill could in turn help educate the public to love beauty. Taking the moral high ground and working so tirelessly for the public good makes it difficult to isolate the private individual behind the slightly pompous, if always sincere, public face. Given the bias of our times it comes as a relief when one finds a more private drawing in which personal charm and wit triumph over the pronouncements of the Public Man. One thing is certain however: it is not the private side of his work on which Crane would wish to be judged.

This said, Crane introduced many personal elements into his work. The Toy Books abound in these, from the use of the family chairs in Beauty and the Beast 1874 (A19) to the silhouettes that hang on the wall in This Little Pig 1870 (A12), which were based on his father's portraits of the Crane family. Annie and Jack in London 1869 (A8) is based on a family outing whilst My Mother 1874 casts his wife, Mary Frances Andrews, in the role of the mother. The 'black books' (A25 and A26), produced to entertain and inform his children, were another area of private work which crossed the public boundary.

Crane's love for Mary also dominated his exhibited work for several years after they first met. At Home 1872 (D3, plate IV) and A Herald of Spring 1872 (D2, ill p109) both feature her as the model. More unusual was the painting Love's Altar 1870 (D1, ill p15) which shows a pilgrim to the Chapel of Love kneeling in front of an altar adorned with her portrait. Like many Victorian men Crane wished to announce publicly his private joys, whether his love for his wife or the pattern of domestic harmony with which he sought to surround himself.

The question of the merging of public and private in Crane's work would be of limited interest were it not for the emphasis placed in Crane's theoretical writings on a different distinction. 'Painting', Crane wrote, 'becomes

more and more a matter of individual expression or impression, and modern economic and commercial conditions favour this individualism'.[1] He believed that 'The decline of art corresponds with its conversion into portable forms of private property, or material or commercial speculation',[2] and that all truly great works of art 'are public' which, since they are the product of a unified society, are 'the art of the people'. The Gothic Cathedral was the true pattern of public art, not the illustrated magazine, which, though bought in bulk, was produced by the few.

The implications of such a distinction are important: it suggests that, in Crane's eyes, much of what he produced fits his definition of 'private' and fails to live up to his highest ideals. Crane would argue that that was the fate of any artist working within Capitalism since not only were public commissions unforthcoming, but art was bought and sold like any other commodity and must therefore first satisfy the private tastes of the purchaser. The other implication of Crane's belief in the necessity of a public art is that what we now see as a tendency to simplistic symbolism was originally conceived as an attempt to create a secular language of public art which all could understand. Symbolism if it was hermetic and painting if it was expressive were, according to Crane, private in the sense that they said too much about the individual and not enough about Man. Such a distinction was based on the ideal that art is, or should be, 'the language of … a universal feeling which [is], shared more or less by all, consciously or unconsciously'.[3] Artists must, thought Crane, be a part of society which they have a duty to serve. The artist is special only in that art may be 'fully comprehended, passionately expressed, and communicated in tangible and eloquent shape by comparatively few'.[4] The prime responsibility is thus not to celebrate this uniqueness, but to bridge the gap and this required an art which spoke to all, and of matters which concerned all.

Crane faced two principal problems in the pursuit of this goal: how to evolve a language which was generally intelligible but was not dependent either on overtly religious symbols or on conventions discredited by a comp-

Walter Crane & *Walruses* (A25ii)

licity with Capitalism, and how to find a subject-matter which, though it eschewed religion and the Christian virtues, did not abandon morality as its foundation. In both of these areas Crane's ideas on Nature were very important.

The symbolic language of nature

Crane's response to landscape was always intense, but whereas his early work expressed this in terms of a Pre-Raphaelite attention to detail his work in the 1870s and 1880s, showed a growing dissatisfaction with what he called 'literalism'. The symbolic language he used, however, although no less passionately felt, now seems a poor reflection of the beauties and mystery which he wished to celebrate. Konody's view that the 'continual, almost mechanical, repetition of certain types ... degenerating ... into mere symbols'[5] was detrimental to his work, is widely shared. Such a charge, however, puts an undue stress on the aesthetic. Crane's response to Konody would have been to agree; 'symbols' and 'types' were just what he wished to create. What we need to understand is why?

The first signs of a tension between the naturalistic and the symbolic occurred towards the end of the 1860s and appear as a clear dichotomy in those works executed in Italy, 1871-3. Landscapes capturing the beauty of Rome in spring and the Italian countryside, such as *Vietri on the Gulf of Salerno* (C17, ill p16), exist next to more public works in which the same themes are explored in symbolic terms. This set the pattern for the rest of Crane's career as a landscape artist, a naturalistic approach for the private medium of watercolour and a symbolic mode for a public statement in oil or tempera. Works such as *A Herald of Spring* 1872 (D2, ill p109), however, achieve a sense of balance between the universal and the particular. This was easier to maintain when the allegory or subject was rooted in a sense of place. Thus concurrent with an abstract conception of nature as in *The Renascence of Venus* 1882 (D4, ill p19), one also finds, as late as 1881, in *The Laidley Worm of Spindleton Heugh* (ill p16), a public subject painting which, because of its genesis in a response to an actual place, Bamborough (Bamburgh) Castle in Northumberland (C25) gains a greater power in spite of its romantic subject.

The move to a symbolic conception of nature was, as is often the case with Crane, a result of his need to intellectualise the subject, in this case man's relationship with his environment. A study of classical history, archaeology and the origin of religions led Crane to the view, widely held in Rationalist circles, that a 'foundation of natural mythology was common to them all', and that early religions were 'nothing but figurative systems – personifications and symbols of the forces of nature'.[6] Crane believed that an art which was universal, which cut across time and expressed broad truths must be founded on a 'succinct language' of 'pictorial emblem, symbol, or allegory' which alone 'can express some sense of the great powers of nature'.[7]

This is the elevated theory which lay behind Crane's repetitions of *The Seasons*, *Times of Day*, *The Elements* etc, all personified as their Latin, Italian or French gender required, as idealised women. It is the basis too of the string of allegorical paintings on the theme of Nature. There was, however, a difference between the decorative use of a repertoire of symbolic motifs which have lost much of their meaning, and the use of the same symbols in painting. In the 'decorative arts' they are made acceptable by Crane's abstract, pattern-making ability; this does not have the same force in the paintings. They may display a decorative sense but, without the attractions of bravura handling and bold colouring, qualities (or distractions)

Walter Crane *Love's Altar* (D1)

Top
Walter Crane *Vietri on the Gulf of Salerno* (C17)

Bottom
Walter Crane *The Laidley Worm of Spindleton Heugh* 1881, oil.
Rothschild Collections Ltd

which Crane deliberately eschewed, the simplistic allegories on their own offer little interest. The power of art to engage is partly dependent on ambiguity and that is something which Crane's aesthetic had no room for.

Crane's belief that the symbolic mode was superior because it was the product of the imagination and the poetic impulse, not observation, was one of the ways in which he was influenced by William Blake. Crane's description of his love of a symbolism which 'hangs the mind's house with a mysterious tapestry of figurative thoughts, a rich and fantastic imagery, a world where the elements are personified, where every tree has its dryad' is resonant of Blake.[8] His assertion, made later in his career, that 'an artist works most freely and best without any direct reference to nature and should have learned by heart the forms he makes use of'[9] is again more Blake than Ruskin. The illustrated poem, *The Sirens Three* 1885 (A38), was also conceived as a parallel to Blake's prophetic books.

The major difficulty in appreciating Crane's use of symbolism, in *The Triumph of Spring* 1879 (ill p18) is accepting the simplicity of such a conception, for however much Crane was influenced by Blake his imagination still worked on a prosaic level. The problem though is not unique to this century, as his limited commercial success suggests. Though Crane regarded that as evidence only of a more universal validity, it does, however, underline the paradox of attempting to formulate a public language for an undemocratic branch of the arts: he could reach only the wealthy and sophisticated few who visited exhibitions.

Another problem with Crane's symbolism is that it was, and still is, easy to dismiss as escapist. Crane believed that art is a reflection of the society that produces it and that, given the nature of contemporary life, art can either be bad, in the sense that it reflects the materialistic, individualistic basis of that society, or sordid and negative in its naturalistic representation of its evils. Crane saw a need for the exposure of social problems but believed that 'people will not be satisfied with destructiveness'. He felt the need, instead, to show 'the search for a new harmony, a higher sense of beauty'.[10] Crane's concept of a public language based on a complex analysis of the continuity of allegory, the primacy of Nature, and on the need for 'a higher sense of beauty' meant the artist addressed only an elite who shared his ideals. Crane understood the problem but would have been disappointed that his works had not helped to educate people to create a society, which, through its public affiliations, would have created the terms of reference which would allow his concept of art to be universally accepted.

Walter Crane *Nox* (Night) (K6iv)

At the same time Crane, as an active socialist, evolved a parallel, more populist approach to the symbolic representation of nature. The revival of the folk tradition of the celebration of May Day and the grafting onto it of a political meaning gave Crane an attractive image of social unity, of workers dancing around the May Pole. In the cartoon *The Triumph of Labour* 1891 (B8, ill p18) he also adapted the imagery of the Triumph and turned it into a procession of the workers of the world. The celebration of the renewal of the seasons gave to the workers' struggle something of the historic inevitability fundamental to Marxist thought, without any hint of violent struggle.

Another exception to the problematic use of natural symbolism was *The Horses of Neptune* 1892 (ill p19). Crane's account of its conception is an interesting example of the genesis of a subject. The first idea was characteristically linguistic: 'I had been accustomed to hear the waves spoken of as "white horses", and the idea seemed to be a perfectly natural and familiar one'. Often with Crane the thinking did not get beyond this simplistic level; thus the flower books often contain no more than a series of visual puns on the flowers' common names. In this case, however, observation of nature played its part. Crane tells how he saw 'the wind often catching the crests of the waves just as they curled over to break, and blowing the spray out like the mane of prancing steeds – the motive sug-

Top
Walter Crane *The Triumph of Spring* 1879, tempera. National
Museums on Merseyside, Walker Art Gallery

Bottom
Walter Crane *The Triumph of Labour*, from 'Cartoons for the Cause' (B8)

gested itself.'[11] The result was an image which is closer to
the ideal of universality since it was rooted in a common
experience of nature.

Walter Crane and the theory of progress

Well before his adoption of Socialism in the mid-1880s
Crane underwent a philosophical conversion just as profound and one which was to make possible the later commitment. According to the *Reminiscences* it was J R Wise who
introduced Crane to the writings of Emerson and thus
'helped to clear my mind from superstitious shadows and
theological bogies which at one time rather oppressed

me'.[12] From the mid-1860s Crane read increasingly
widely and noted passages from writers such as 'J S Mill,
Darwin, Herbert Spencer'.[13] It is characteristic of Crane,
however, that it should have been a poet, Shelley, rather
than a philosopher, who had the greatest influence on his
decision to opt for 'Free Thought'. Ruskin was also
important. *The Seven Lamps of Architecture* introduced Crane to
ideas such as truth to material and the dignity of labour
and the social ideals of *Unto This Last* prepared the way for
Crane's decisive and long-lasting commitment to the
ideals of William Morris.

   It was, however, the evolutionist theories of Auguste
Comte which had the most interesting effects on Crane's

Top
Walter Crane *The Horses of Neptune* 1892, oil. Neue Pinakothek, Munich

Bottom
Walter Crane *The Renascence of Venus* (D4)

Walter Crane *The Bridge of Life* 1884, oil. Untraced

thinking. Comte believed in the primacy of reason and in
the importance of history in determining the affairs of
man. His three-stage model of social development began
with the 'theological' stage, equivalent to the natural religion which Crane had identified with early personifications of the elements. The next was the 'metaphysical'
which saw the dominance of organised religion. This was
followed inexorably by the final 'positive' stage at which
point the application of reason leads to the understanding
that Man, not God, is the true source of religion. A con-
comitant belief was that Man evolves from the pursuit of
self-interest towards a social unity.

Crane's interest in evolutionist theories also took in the
writings of Charles Darwin. Crane's view that art is 'an
organic thing , having its own laws … is a result of that
continual fierce and strenuous struggle for existence
throughout nature'[14] is based on Darwin's theory of
natural selection. So too is a belief that decorative forms
evolve and that one could 'classify patterns into species
and genera'.[15] But Crane's knowledge of art meant that a
simplistic evolutionary reading of art and social progress

was impossible; the available evidence suggested that it
was the seasons which offered the better model and that
both had their 'own ever-recurring seasons – growth, per-
fection, decline, and renaissance'.[16] Thus though Comte's
ideas gave cause for optimism, as did Socialism, Nature
was as instructive as philosophy. *The Renascence of Venus* 1877
(D4, ill p19) is to be understood in these terms; the
rebirth of beauty is related to the regeneration of the
seasons.

The progress of mankind, however, was more difficult
to show. *The Bridge of Life* 1884 (ill p20) could show the
stages of man's journey through life (though it required
a long written explanation), but human perfectability,
rather than *The Progress of Locomotion* (ill p53), lay in taking
a step back. Progress stemmed not from isolated discov-
eries, but the 'collective experience of ages'. Change,
according to Crane, is due to 'continuity of custom, life,
and habit, and the continuous associated labour of communities, wherein the individual is of less importance than
the maintenance of the social organism'.[17] The genius,
'become[s] what [he is] because of an existing vital tradit-

Walter Crane *The Sirens Three, Stanza LXXII* (A38)

ion admitting of individual variation'.[18] Given this interpretation, which minimises the role of the individual, it is hardly surprising that the multitude is represented in Crane's work by the ideal type, and that progress is reduced to the repetition of the symbolic triumph: St George's over the dragon.

The clearest embodiment of Crane's evolutionist ideals is the poem *The Sirens Three* 1885 (A38) which, because it was illustrated, has generally been commented on only in the context of its decoration. It opens with a description of a vain search for 'Truth' in a wasteland of 'shattered caskets of man's winged brain', the ruined churches, temples of organised religion. Seeking an explanation the poet enters 'Time's House' and there sees the story of Man unfolding: 'Long his descent, his pedigree obscure'. After Man's 'savage infancy' comes the birth of 'Thought and Art, Man's children fair' and thus begins the Golden Age. In Crane's eyes the Fall occurs when 'Fear and Ignorance' gain the upper hand and man is bound a slave 'Between the soldier-king & priest of old' (A38, ill p21). Here he remains: 'Till Nature roused him from his dreams again,/

And Reason broke the chains'. The conclusion is optimistic and affirms the positive role of science within a socialist future. According to the poem Nature and Reason are the twin pillars of society, progress and the passing of the seasons are its primary mechanisms and Socialism and science are its guarantees of a glorious future.

Socialism and the 'unity of public sentiment'

The Claims of Decorative Art 1892 contains a series of essays which were the direct outcome of Crane's espousal of Socialism and include the fullest analysis of his understanding of the links between art and society. In particular Crane developed his ideas about the need for an 'equality and unity of all art-workers'.[19] This was essential, not just to improve standards of design and production, but, and this is where Crane caused dissent, it was also to be a pattern for the reconstruction of the basis of society. Following Morris, the arts were to have a 'primal unity in architecture' but that within 'this fraternal unity none is before or after the other'.[20]

The issue of how individuality should relate to unity was important to Crane and one which demanded a practical solution in art teaching which had to be varied and responsive if it was not to turn the student into an automaton. Crane's answer was that individuality depended on social structure. Within Capitalism it led to competition and specialisation. The only hope lay in the 'new ideal' of Socialism, 'a religion and a moral code as well as an economic system. Its true realization would mean once again that unity of public sentiment.'[21] This alone could ensure 'no dead level of uniformity but that comprehensive and harmonizing unity with individual variety'. The distinction between public and private was dissolved in an ideal situation in which the agglomerate voice of individuals, united in a 'Commonweal', creates a new 'vernacular in art'.[22]

'Public' was, however, more likely to mean 'in the public eye' and Crane was typical of his generation in his adherence to an ideology of public service, whereby men who had achieved status within their profession took on a variety of honorary roles. Although snubbed by the establishment Crane was, in this respect, no different from other members of the professional classes. Although in theory opposed to art teaching outside the workshop, Crane worked energetically from within established institutions to effect change. He illustrated a Board of Education report on primary school drawing, acted as an examiner for the National Art Training School and helped organise the British contribution to international exhibitions in Paris and Turin.

Crane's interest in teaching also led him to accept official posts in the Art Colleges he disapproved of. Beginning an article 'Of the Teaching of Art' with the statement 'You cannot teach it',[23] Crane demonstrates the ambiguity of his position. He was prepared to accept that if one 'endeavour[s] to teach relatively',[24] by which he meant each of the arts in relation to each other, and by 'demonstration, always demonstration',[25] there was some point to art education. As a Fabian, by nature as well as affili-

ation, Crane took the view that education, not revolution, was the main way forward. But until the workshop actually replaced the Municipal Art College, all was by necessity compromise: good art, he argued, is 'an outcome and efflorescence of the delight in life under happy conditions'[26] and 'if we take care of life, art will take care of itself.'[27]

Having looked at the problems which beset the pursuit of a public art there were two areas of Crane's work which were able to bypass high art and thus address people more directly; both arose from his work as a socialist. Crane was no great orator and his lectures were addressed to small audiences but, as those who attended testified, he was marvellously eloquent when he began to draw. Crane's belief that 'no touch or conception of life but is made more emphatic and comprehensible by being cast into a concrete image'[28] and the skills he had acquired as a children's book illustrator in making the complex intelligible, particularly suited him for the role of artist for the socialist cause. His ideas on allegory also bore fruit: 'Allegorical art has, too, a modern popular form in the region of political satire and caricature'.[29] In the cartoons he produced for Justice, The Daily Chronicle and others he developed a crude, but effective, cast of allegorical types: Liberty, Labour (B8, ill p88), Peace, Capitalism, Imperialism etc which, when combined with topical captions, conveyed simple truths in a way which was appropriate to the ephemeral newspaper medium.

Crane's definition of a public art also included the large-scale mural decoration of public buildings. Apart from the murals Crane executed for the Royal West of England Academy, illustrating The Arts, his large-scale decorative projects were confined to private houses. An exception to this were the murals he designed for the Red Cross Hall, Southwark 1891 (ill p23). This was the nearest Crane got to fulfilling a long cherished idea: 'if education was considered … as a means of developing the whole nature … might we not, from the storehouse of history and folklore, picture our school and college walls with great and typical figures of heroes, and founders and fighters for our liberties and the commonwealth'.[30] The fourth Arts and Crafts Exhibition included 'Spring, Seed-Time and Summer - Cartoons for a scheme of printed decoration for school walls' but nothing seems to have come of it. Red Cross Hall suffered similar problems without the enlightened official support which had realised Ford Madox Brown's murals in Manchester Town Hall.

The portrayal of working-class heroes to decorate a hall built to serve the tenants of 'industrial dwellings' as a

Walter Crane *The Worker's Maypole*, from 'Cartoons for the Cause' (B8)

'reading-room, gymnasium, and concert hall'[31] was the outcome of Crane's meeting with Octavia Hill. The design of the building brings to mind Crane's call for designs for communal living based on the medieval college[32] and this is married to a philanthropic desire to provide a healthy diet of exercise for mind and body. The existence of a number of life studies for one of only two scenes completed, *Alice Ayres* (C35, ill p107) suggests that the exceptional circumstances of painting a scene of contemporary life forced Crane to adopt a more naturalistic approach.

This remained, however, an exception. Crane believed that:

'When the artist desires to soar a little above the passing moment to suggest the past, to peer into the future; when he looks at human life as a complete whole, and the life of the race as an unbroken chain; when he would deal with the thoughts of

man's origin and destiny, of the powers and passions that sway him, of loves, of hope and fear, of the mystery of life and nature, the drama of the seasons, he must use figurative language, and seek the beautiful and permanent images of emblematic design.'[33]

These were the proper subjects for a public art and the only language to express them in was allegorical.

Notes

1   Crane, *Reminiscences* pp297–8
2   Crane, *Claims* p16
3   Ibid p124
4   Ibid
5   Konody p27
6   Crane, *Claims* p23
7   Crane, *Bases* p215
8   Crane, *Line* p222
9   Konody p110
10 Crane, *Reminiscences* p336
11 Ibid p408
12 Ibid p78
13 Ibid p80
14 Crane, *Claims* p3
15 Ibid p47
16 Ibid p3
17 Crane, *Bases* p337
18 Ibid p343
19 Crane, *Claims* Preface
20 Ibid
21 Ibid p79
22 Ibid p80
23 Crane, *Ideals* p35
24 Ibid p52
25 Ibid p44
26 Ibid p36
27 Ibid p56
28 Crane, *Claims* p29
29 Crane, *Bases* p249
30 Crane, *Ideals* p98
31 *The Builder* 1889 pp331–2
32 Crane, *Ideals* p117
33 Crane, *Bases* p249

The Interior of the Red Cross Hall, Southwark, from 'The Builder' 1889

Sarah Hyde

The Production of Walter Crane's Children's Books

Crane devoted remarkably little space in his *Reminiscences* to his work as a designer of book illustrations, betraying some anxiety that his reputation should be founded on what he thought of as his 'more ambitious' work – his paintings.[1] By 1913 he realised he was fighting a losing battle, although he still found it difficult to accept that, of all his myriad activities, it was one which he considered among the least significant for which he was most celebrated: 'I was labelled designer of childrens' books long ago – although designs for children's books, strictly speaking, have only formed a comparatively small part of my work.'[2]

Crane's reputation in the 1980s is still based as strongly as ever on his 'book-work'. Book production is, however, by its very nature, a co-operative effort. The final image on the printed page is not merely the result of various influences on Crane's drawing style; it depends equally on his complex working relationships with printers, engravers and publishers, and on the technical developments which, during his working life, radically changed the way in which images could be printed. This essay will, therefore, focus on the circumstances surrounding the production of 'Walter Crane's' picture books: the changing working relations and technical developments which created the books, and in particular on the part played by Edmund Evans' engraving and printing workshop. There has been a tendency in recent years to see the success of Evans' work with Crane as being based on their ability to exploit the simple strengths of wood-engraving at a time when this process was rapidly being overtaken by more advanced and more cost-effective methods of printing book illustrations.[3] In fact, both Crane and Evans' attitudes towards these new processes, and the use they made of them in their work, were more complicated than this would suggest.

Crane's attitude towards his work as an illustrator of children's books and his uneasy relationships with their publishers, were shaped partly by his ambiguous attitude towards the idea of his work being controlled by commercial calculation. Initially, the arrangement Crane made with Routledge as publishers of Toy Books was that his

drawings were sold outright, for a one-off 'modest sum',[4] the commercial speculation and potential profit or loss on sales being entirely the publisher's. Later, once his Toy Books had proved a commercial success, and were being listed separately from Routledge's other Toy Books as 'Walter Crane's New Series', Crane wanted to be paid a royalty, and was annoyed when the publisher refused to agree.[5] However, although he wanted a share of the profits, Crane was nonetheless the first to complain if it seemed that profit was the sole motivating force. He was convinced that the new style of design and printing which he and Evans had introduced into their Toy Books was a great improvement over other work being produced in this field. He felt, therefore, that it was their obsession with commercial gain which prevented Routledge from giving his work the support and appreciation it deserved: 'the publishers ... thought the raw, coarse colours, and vulgar designs usually current appealed to a larger public, and therefore paid better'.[6] Likewise, when asked by Routledge to produce a follow up to the commercially very successful *The Baby's Opera* 1877 (A22, plate I, ill p79), he refused 'not wishing to produce a less spontaneous book simply to meet commercial demands'.[7] Crane's relations with publishers worsened as several either issued collections or compilations of his works without consulting him, or, as in the case of Kate Greenaway's *Under the Window* 1878, used his name to promote sales of another book without his permission. The negotiations he entered into with Routledge during the mid-1890s in order to purchase the printing blocks of the sixpenny Toy Books further demonstrate Crane's growing distrust of publishers, and the lengths to which he would go in order to control the appearance of work published under his name.[8] He wrote feelingly of an imagined medieval past 'when time was no object and the pious artist and scribe could work quietly and lovingly to make a thing of beauty with no fear of a publisher or a printer before his eyes, or the demands of a world market.'[9]

Crane was not, however, always directly responsible to a publishing house for his work; early in his career he frequently worked to the directions of an engraving and printing establishment such as Linton's or Evans'. However, this did not mean that, as a young draughtsman at least, he was in any less subservient a position. Letters written to Crane by Linton's partner, Orrin Smith, show that it paid the proprietor of an engraving workshop to exert detailed control over the productions of draughtsmen from whom he commissioned work. Orrin Smith wrote on one of Crane's drawings:

'The man on left hand will look like a black beetle when engraved. Please give yr figures neater definition, I would rather pay more for the drawing as I can save it on the engraving and make a better block'[10]

For the early Toy Books, it was Evans who directed Crane's work, although publishers such as Warne's still retained ultimate control, and evidently made that quite clear; Crane writes:

'I certainly remember this firm requesting (through Mr Edmund Evans, the engraver and printer who sent me the work), that some children I designed for another book "should not be unnecessarily covered with hair" – long hair being at the time a dangerous innovation of pre-Raphaelite tendency.'[11]

Evans' role in the production of books varied a great deal. Anyone with a workshop the size of his to run (he employed as many as thirty people during the 1860s and 1870s)[12] had to maintain some independence from publishers in order to keep the work flowing in. This involved working simultaneously for rival publishers, as well as commissioning work independently of publishers. In 1867 he wrote to Crane:

'I cannot get Routledge to look at the toy book or anything for which you made sketches, they say they will not 'till after Christmas. However I am so short of work for some of my engravers I will venture on one of them. I think the Grammar the safest.'[13]

The shilling Toy Books were likewise a venture of Evans' rather than Routledge.[14] Evans stockpiled sheets already printed with illustrations for the books, which he would then sell to publishers who would bind them and issue them as subsequent editions as demand dictated. The initial decision as to how many copies were to be printed seems frequently to have been made by Evans rather than Routledge, although George Routledge often disputed Evans' judgement. Evans recalled that he was 'chaffed … considerably'[15] for printing 20,000 copies of a book by a new author to sell at 6s per copy – Kate Greenaway's *Under the Window*. As his career progressed, however, Evans was willing to speculate more heavily on publications; with one of Caldecott's books, for example 'I agreed to

run all the risk of engraving the key blocks which he drew on wood … I was to supply paper, and print 10,000 copies, which George Routledge & Sons have published for me.'[16] Acting thus independently Evans would have to stand the loss of books which did not sell. Occasionally he betrayed some annoyance at this position. For Kate Greenaway's first two books, Evans had to pay her a share of the profits as well as paying for her drawings. However, in 1855, when her *English Spelling Book* did not sell, Evans had to take the loss, whereas Greenaway was not only paid for her work but also had her original drawings returned to her after they were printed.

Evans' work with Crane made up only a small part of the output of his establishment. The bulk of his work continued to be the production of book covers and basic two- or three-colour printing for publishers, a distinction Crane makes as between 'choice books' and 'ordinary trade work'.[17] It is, however, important not to underestimate the contribution which Evans made to what are normally described as 'Crane's Toy Books'. The choice and balance of colours for the illustrations, on which the success of the books depends so heavily, was clearly to a large extent Evans' work; as Crane admits 'Mr Evans was not only a man of business but a clever artist in watercolour himself, and aided my efforts in the direction of more tasteful colouring in children's books.'[18] Although Evans does not seem to have done much engraving himself after the 1850s, he still maintained detailed control over the planning and cutting of lines by his employees: 'I had to direct the engravers even to the direction of the lines in the colour blocks.' Similarly, the all-important decisions as to the choice and mixing of inks were his: 'I had to direct the printers in the tones of the inks for printing, after mixing the inks.'[19]

During Crane's lifetime, however, new technology in the printing trade had drastic effects on the structure of the working relations described above. The craft in which Crane was apprenticed as a youth, for example, that of a 'draughtsman on wood', was to become obsolete during the course of his working life, replaced by photography.[20] It has been common for authors from Martin Hardie onwards to see Evans' work as somehow resisting the advance of new technology; Hardie praised Evans' work for its purity of line and simplicity of flat tints, and saw the reproduction of Crane's designs in other media by other printers and publishers, such as *The Three R's* 1886 (A27-A29), and *Queen Summer* 1891 (A35)) as abandoning this 'purity' for 'elaborate colour effects'.[21] However, some of Evans' and Crane's greatest successes, such as the shilling Toy Books, were in fact based on the most elaborate colour effects achieved by great complexity of cutting and overprinting. Evans himself, while never wholly abandoning his love of the crispness of wood-engraved lines, was clearly not as unwilling as has previously been thought to experiment in mixing them with newly-developed techniques to achieve tone and texture in relief printing. A brief analysis, in chronological order, of three examples of the growing complexity of Evans' work followed by a discussion of both Crane and Evans' attitude towards new technology in printing, and examples of Evans' use of certain new techniques, will make this point. Unfortunately, the crispness of Evans' wood-engraved lines cannot be fully conveyed by the four-colour half-tone process used to print the colour plates in this book; the clearest idea of Evans' techniques can only be gained by studying the books themselves.

For the production of book covers during the early 1860s, Evans himself was responsible for deciding where and how to apply the colour blocks:

'The artists of the day were asked to supply drawings which were engraved on wood: then two "transfers" from the engraved block, ie impressions while wet laid face down on plain blocks, then put through the press so that the wet impression was "set off" on the plain blocks, and used, one for a Red printing, the others for a Blue printing, the red being engraved in graduation to get the light tints, such as faces, hands, etc – the Blue block being engraved to get the best result of texture, patterns of sky, crossing the blue over the red to get good effects of light and shade ... There were generally only three printings used – black, blue and red, or black, green and red.'[22]

Although the early Toy Books, such as Sing a Song of Sixpence 1866 (A7) were printed in a similar manner, surviving preparatory drawings suggest that for these books Crane took more of the decisions as to how the colour was to be applied. He adopted a rather conservative approach: shadows are suggested mainly by areas of black cross hatching, with the blue and red used mainly to suggest local colour (ill p27). The colours are applied flat in some areas, such as the full red of the Queen's skirt, or cut into lines with the graver in others, for example to give the effect of pink for her face. There is some overprinting – lines are printed on top of flat red for the woman's jacket – but Evans has not managed to use this to introduce a new colour; the result is not purple but merely a darker blue.

Three years later, as the plate from 1, 2, Buckle My Shoe 1869 (A10, ill p28) demonstrates, Evans' colour printing looks notably more sophisticated. This is only partly because the number of colours printed has increased to five. It is also due to the colours being used in a different way. Shadows, such as that cast by the table top into the drawer below, are now described in colour rather than with cross-hatched black lines. The earlier style of pen drawing has been given up completely, under, as Crane stressed, the influence of Japanese woodblock prints. Nonetheless, the actual manner of cutting the woodblocks with the graver is still very restrained, consisting mostly of simple parallel lines cut with a tint tool, usually running either vertically or diagonally across the printed page. By the time Crane and Evans were working independently on the production of books such as The Baby's Opera 1877 (A22), the sophistication of the cutting and colour printing had increased dramatically (plate I). The blue stockings worn by the fiddlers are the only flat colours printed. All other areas of colour are textured by various patterns cut into the wooden block, and the subtlety of the final range of visible colour depends as much on these textures as it does on the overprinting and the choice of inks. For example, the range of browns in the picture is created not only by overlaying different colours but by laying the colours on in different textures. The first fiddler's hair consists of red lines and blue dots, the second of red lines crossed by blue lines; the warm brown of the violins is made by thicker red lines over blue dots, whilst Old King Cole's robes are made from variations of red lines and blue dots printed over a flat yellow ground.

The illustrations for the shilling Toy Book, Aladdin; or The Wonderful Lamp 1875 (A20, plate IX on front cover), although printed two years before The Baby's Opera, are an even more impressive tour de force of colour printing. Here Evans exploits not only the colour-printed wood engraved lines, but also the white spaces between those lines, cutting the blocks in such a way as to use the effect of the colours to be printed underneath the line-block which will show through in these white spaces. The choice of colours in Aladdin also suggests that Evans had not printed the colour plates to Routledge's edition of Maurice Chevreul's The Laws of Contrast of Colour 1861 without taking some heed of Chevreul's theories. Chevreul's own researches into colour theory were conducted for practical reasons, stemming from his work as Director of the dye works for the Gobelins tapestry workshop. He believed that contiguous colours, when looked at together, have a modifying effect on each other; modifications which he formulated as the law of simultaneous contrast of colours. Although too complex to go into here, his theories suggest

Walter Crane Page from 'Sing a Song of Sixpence' (A7)

Walter Crane *Page from '1, 2, Buckle My Shoe'* (A10)

that 'the modifications of contiguous colours are ... those that would result from the addition to each of them of the complementary of the contiguous colour.'[23] Therefore, when two complementary colours are placed side by side, the intensity of each colour is increased at the points where they meet. The vibrancy of the orange of Aladdin's robes has accordingly been created by surrounding the orange by as many areas as possible of its contrasting colour, blue. Chevreul also experimented with the effects of black on contiguous colours, concluding that black next to orange made the orange more brilliant. The black outlines around Aladdin's orange drapery show this effect; Chevreul's theories would have given encouragement to a tendency in Crane's drawing style towards the use of strong black outline around his figures, initially adopted in imitation of Japanese prints. Some of the illustrations to Chevreul's book demonstrate the varying effects of mixing strands of two different colours of wool in different ratios; the similarity between these lines of coloured wool and the lines cut by the wood-engraver suggest that Evans may have made use of Chevreul's theories in the more detailed mixing of overprinted colours as well as in the larger effects of juxtaposed areas of colours.

As already mentioned, the effect of these colours on the eye depends as much on the textural treatment of the relief surfaces from which they were printed as on the choice of colours to be juxtaposed or superimposed. Although the prints in Crane and Evans' books are normally described as 'wood-engravings', the surface from which they were printed would almost always have been metal rather than wood. From the mid-nineteenth century on most wood-engravings were printed from metal duplicates of the wooden blocks made by electrotyping, mainly to avoid the dangers of the wood splitting during the course of a long print run. During the middle years of the nineteenth century, however, several colour printers experimented not only with metal 'stereos' of wooden blocks, but with relief blocks made by painting the design to be printed onto metal in some form of resin, and then etching away the surrounding areas.[24] Once it had been proved possible to use transfer paper to create these acid-resistant areas on the metal block, the way was open to a whole variety of manufactured textural effects which could be created on the transfer paper and then etched in relief on the metal block, ultimately preparing the way for the photographic line-block. Bamber Gascoigne has revived the use of the word 'chromotypography' to describe 'any colour relief print in which some or all of the

Walter Crane *Page from 'Pan Pipes'* (detail) (A33)

colours are printed in variable tones from metal blocks';[25] the word is indeed a more accurate description than 'wood-engraving' of the way in which Crane and Evans' books were printed during the 1880s, and by Evans' firm into the 1890s (Evans himself retired in 1892). *The Baby's Own Æsop* 1886 (A24) for example, was printed from a combination of line-block and wood-engraving. The tonal areas in many of the illustrations in *Pan Pipes* 1882 (A33, ill p29) were created by transferring the pattern made by reticulated gelatin onto metal plates as an acid resist. The firm also used the texture of linen in a similar way to create a background tone in *Steps to Reading* 1898 (A31i, ill p30).

Walter Crane *Page from 'Steps to Reading'* (A31i)

own text in the character that pleases him, … and so make his page a consistent whole from a decorative point of view.'[27]

In the end, since Crane's drawing style was formed from the beginning with the constraints of printing from engraved woodblocks in mind, his most stringent criticism of photography was not that it produced unattractive prints, but that it fed back into the draughtsman's and illustrator's style, which he saw, at the end of the nineteenth century, becoming adulterated with concerns proper only to the consideration of the painter:

'Its influence, however, on artistic style and treatment has been … of more doubtful advantage. It has led in illustrative work to the method of painting in black and white, which has taken the place very much of the use of line, and through this, and by reason of its having fostered and encouraged a different way of regarding nature – from the point of view of accidental aspect, light and shade, and tone – it has confused and deteriorated, I think, the faculty of inventive design, and the sense of ornament and line; having concentrated artistic interest on the literal realization of certain aspects of superficial facts, and instantaneous impressions instead of ideas, and the abstract treatment of form and line.'[28]

Notes

1   Crane, *Reminiscences* p178
2   Crane, *Imprint* p81
3   Eg Joan Friedman, *Colour Printing in England 1486-1870* Yale Center for British Art, New Haven 1978 p37
4   Crane, *Reminiscences* p156
5   Ibid p178
6   Ibid p76
7   Ibid p180
8   Correspondence between Crane and the publishers John Lane & Co, now housed in the Houghton Library and in the collection of Anthony Crane.
9   Crane, *Decorative Illustration* p26
10   A Crane, *Yale Gazette* p102
11   Crane, *Art Journal* p3
12   See introduction to McLean
13   A Crane, *Yale Gazette* p102
14   See the Houghton Library's correspondence between Crane and John Lane for 1894.
15   McLean p61
16   Ibid p56
17   Crane, *Reminiscences* p74
18   Ibid p76
19   McLean p48
20   Crane, *Reminiscences* p148
21   Martin Hardie, *English Coloured Books* 1906 p275
22   McLean pp26-8
23   Chevreul p8. I am grateful to Paul Smith for suggesting the link between Evans and Chevreul.
24   For example Charles Knight, and several of George Baxter's licensees. Crane also describes experiments made by his master Linton, with a method of printing in relief from metal plates called Kerography (Crane, *Reminiscences* p56).
25   Bamber Gascoigne, *How to Identify Prints* 1986 section 42a
26   W J Linton, *Wood-engraving, A Manual of Instruction* 1884 p52
27   Crane, *Decorative Illustration* p174
28   Ibid p178

One might expect men trained in their youth in printing techniques involving hand drawing and cutting at every stage to resist the gradual move towards mechanism they witnessed during their lifetimes, and in particular the changes caused by the application of photography. Crane, Evans and Linton all recorded their dislike of some of the changes brought about by the increased use of photography. Linton, for example, disliked the substitution of photography for the craft of drawing on the woodblock, although he did admit that he could see a time when line-blocks would replace the function of one aspect of wood-engraving – facsimile work – altogether.[26] Crane likewise could see some advantages in processes such as photogravure used by Goupil and Company to reproduce both text and drawing of *The First of May* 1881 (A37):

'The facile methods of photographic automatic reproduction certainly give an opportunity to the designer to write out his

Joany Hichberger

Walter Crane's Children's Books and Mid-Victorian Attitudes to Childhood

Walter Crane's reworkings of fairy tales and didactic children's stories could only have sprung from mid-Victorian England. His concern with training the child reader for the adult world was part of a network of ideas and beliefs which made childhood a compelling issue in this period. Crane, as artist, illustrator and sometimes writer, was committed to feeding the imagination of his child readers, but beneath the magic and romance of his fairy stories lay a keen desire to utilise the child's leisure time to good effect. These stories are designed to inculcate the values and aspirations of Crane's own social group – the Victorian middle classes. This class, or rather, related network of social groups, saw themselves, and their heirs, as playing a vital role in the continuing economic expansion of the Empire. The Empire was to be remade in the image of British industry, democracy and virtue. Although not as crudely nationalistic as G H Henty's roughly contemporary *Boy's Own* stories, in their own way Crane's books manifest similar concerns. We must not allow Crane's contagious delight in the aesthetic to blind us to the very interesting meanings his stories consciously and unconsciously embody.

Crane's publications for children fall into roughly three categories: the fairy tales often with a letterpress by Crane, the modern stories which were often written by his sister Lucy Crane, and the educational books teaching spelling, grammar and arithmetic which usually included Crane's verses. The educational books seem least likely to provide fruitful study for the student of Victorian social attitudes. Yet even the combination of humour and didacticism is typically Victorian. The Victorian middle classes had recognised that education and self-improvement were the keys to their continued success. The process of moulding the mind and the character were not to be separated however. Learning for its own sake was secondary to learning for the right reasons and learning in the right way. The story of *Little Queen Anne* 1886 (A28, ill p32) is full of heavy puns and humour. The heroine is invited to a ball, for which she dresses as Minerva, Goddess of Wisdom. She meets twenty-six pages (who are both serving-men and book pages), is given lessons in The Three R's by fairy-tale

characters dressed in papers embossed with alphabet letters, and learns languages, geography, science and grammar. The necessity of study for the young is emphasised, ironically, in *The Adventures of Puffy* 1870; the dog, unable to read the warning notice, fell in the lake, 'which shows to all of us what may come if we neglect our reading'.

Despite a concern for moulding children for their roles in the world of the future, Crane's work is redolent of nostalgia. Like Thomas Carlyle and William Morris, he sought to solve contemporary problems by reference to a romanticised past. Crane's choice of 'Golden Ages' seems to have been more aesthetic than political or moral. He believed, for example, that the Middle Ages depicted in *Valentine and Orson* 1874 (A15, ill p75) had been a time of beauty and happiness. He based this view on the 'evidence' of the paintings in brightly coloured, illuminated manuscripts. His was a Middle Ages stripped of war, famine, disease and poverty.

Many of Crane's stories were set in the 'Merrie England' of Good Queen Bess. Elizabeth I's reign was germaine to the Victorians in a number of ways. Then too there had been the long, stable reign of a popular female monarch, when Britain had dominated the seas and acquired valuable foreign lands. Then too enterprise and energy had outweighed aristocratic breeding and traditional privilege. As Roy Strong has shown, the figure of Elizabeth herself was ambiguous: glorious and glamorous yet ill-suited to Victorian ideals of femininity and womanhood.[1] The social and political problems of the past could be cosmeticised more satisfactorily than those of the present. Crane though was wary of the irrationality of the undemocratic past. When Margery is accused of being a witch in *Goody Two Shoes* 1874, having used a barometer to forecast weather, the text, and this is surely Crane, remarks 'Now-a-days it seems strange that such a thing could be; but in England, at that period, so fondly styled by some ''the good old times'', many silly and wicked things were constantly being done, especially by the rich and powerful against the poor – such things as would not now be borne.' Despite this note of caution, *Goody Two Shoes* revels

Walter Crane *Page from 'Little Queen Anne'* (A28)

in a visually delightful mythic England. The Church, symbolising religious piety and order, is at the heart of the village and all types of folk gather together on the pre-Enclosure Acts green. It is an England where the rich voluntarily take responsibility for the welfare of the poor, and where virtuous, charitable bourgeois girls are rewarded for their kindness by marriage to the squire. Margery, 'Goody Two Shoes', sets up a school on the Green (ill p33) and is thus a prototype for the tract-distributing, poor-visiting, wicked-reforming mid-Victorian lady. It is noteworthy that the social injustice which initially reduces the heroine to poverty is perpetrated by a lower-middle-class landlord. The people who rescue Margery are upper-middle-class, the parson and a 'gentleman'. It is as though any class struggle was not between workers and capital, poor and very rich, but between the wicked petty bourgeois against the poor. Crane, and his readers would undoubtedly have identified themselves with the enlightened, beneficent middle classes.

Like many artists in the mid- to late Victorian period, Crane had recourse to the costume and design of the late eighteenth/early nineteenth centuries for inspiration. Their view of this period was, curiously, in almost direct opposition to ours in the late twentieth century. Where

we see the Regency period as more frank than the Victorians about sexual desire and lax in moral attitudes, the mid-Victorians believed that their grandparents had lived in less complex, more innocent times. They particularly believed relations between the sexes had been less dangerously ambiguous. A critic wrote 'Regency genre [painting] has one characteristic which is not found equally in every form of period genre – the inevitability of marriage.'[2] The Regency period was remodelled as a time of simplicity, innocence and glamorous romance by the later nineteenth century. There was a revival of Neo-classical women's fashions and hairstyles of the period c1800-20. Many of the women in Crane's books are the statuesque, large-boned beauties, admired in his own day, wearing either contemporary Aesthetic dress or Regency costume. Both styles of costume of course owed much to the uncorseted drapery of classical antiquity.

In the Romantic period the notion of the child as a natural innocent to be nurtured and protected had evolved. It was the wealthy middle classes of Victorian England who developed the concept economically. The explosion in variety and number of children's toys and games, children's interior design and dress all testify to the Victorian fascination with classifying the mind and interests of the child. For middle-class children, the age of innocence was preserved much longer than for their working-class counterparts. It must be stated, though, that the belief in the sanctity of childhood which had emerged in the mid- to late eighteenth century, slowly resulted in legislation to keep poor children out of the chimneys and coal mines. The world of working-class children who started work, at least part time, before they reached their teens, was removed from the middle-class child's nursery (ill p34) for which Crane's delightful fantasies were intended. Even without the psychological gulf which clearly existed, the shilling or sixpence required to purchase most of the books was far beyond the means of families whose average income in the 1880s was less than 30s per week.[3]

Crane's books represent urban middle class adults' fantasies of life. There is a noticeable lack of wild or rural scenes, with heavy emphasis on the delights of the cultivated, gardened aspects of nature: South Kensington often features in the tales of contemporary life. In *How Jessie Was Lost* 1868, the child strays in the comparative safety of Kensington Gardens before being rescued by a very respectable member of the lower classes, the Park Keeper. Predictably perhaps, the wild in Crane's art is almost always the site of anxiety and lack of security. The children

Walter Crane *Page from 'Goody Two Shoes'* 1874, wood-engraving.
Hornby Library, Liverpool City Libraries

Walter Crane *Page from 'The Baby's Bouquet'* (A23)

in *Annie and Jack in London* 1869 (A8) come up from the suburbs to taste the delights of the city – the zoo, the theatres, shops etc.[4] Again it is a very safe, controlled view of city life. Crane's drawings of the river and cityscapes rigorously exclude smogs, litter, unruly jostling crowds or the fact that the children would most certainly not be able to walk safely without an escort.

If the stories of contemporary life always show a protected and safe world, the fairy tales inevitably involved Crane in negotiating violence and to some extent sexuality. It is well known that many fairy tales are full of the kind of violence which would be banned from contemporary children's television. Crane was fascinated by fairy tales, believing them to embody ancient and universal truths: 'if we could trace the old folk tales back to their sources we might find them all related to primitive mythology or to hero or ancestor worship. Thus do the spirits of the remote past sit at our firesides still, and kindle the imaginations of our little folks: and in the rich tapestry of story and picture which each age weaves around it, elements from many different sources are continually and almost inextricably interwoven ... '[5] In *Little Red Riding Hood* 1875, the wolf swallows the grandmother before being shot by a passing sportsman. Crane evidently decided to evade a more macabre but ancient version of the tale, in which both the grandmother and Red Riding Hood herself

are swallowed by the wolf but are cut from his belly by the woodman's axe. Although Crane consistently referred to the imagination-provoking aspect of fairy stories he liked to keep to logical explanations and happy endings, where the two were compatible.

Crane's version of *Bluebeard* 1875 (ill p35) does not seek to bowdlerise the violence of the original versions. The room forbidden to the curious bride is covered in blood and Bluebeard's former (dead) wives are hung on the walls. The bride is rescued by her brothers, who kill Bluebeard and with typical fairy-story insouciance and amorality, they all live happily ever after in the villain's beautiful palace upon his vast riches.

The mid- to late Victorian middle-class home was a shrine to womanly virtues. The middle-class woman was venerated as both practical home maker/house keeper and as spiritual comforter and inspiration to the man of the house. Womanliness was being constantly reviewed and redefined in this period, as was manliness. An integral part of womanliness was a new emphasis on ladies having more to do with the rearing of their own children. In the eighteenth century, any woman with pretensions to gentility consigned the feeding and early education of her children to servants. In the Victorian period mothering became an attractive, even an erotic occupation for women in male eyes. In this period there was an increase of images of mothers and babies in academic art.

With ladies moving back into the nursery, the nursery became a more design-conscious part of the house. In Crane's illustrations the nursery is a place in which motherliness could be displayed to great advantage. It is important to remember that Crane's books were as much designed for parents as children. On an obvious level it was the parents, possibly the mother, who would buy the books for the nursery. The books then inevitably fed the parents' own sense of well-being about themselves as wise, nurturing, capable, omniscient beings. *My Mother* 1873 shows a wonderfully glamorous mother, with modish aesthetic dress and classical hairstyle. The rather unctuous little rhyme features an equally smart nursery, with French Empire-style tiles, wallpaper and carpets. The first part of *My Mother* extolls the selfless devotion of the mother who fed, nursed and played with the child, but the end of the story has a rather grim warning not to neglect aged parents:

'For GOD, who lives about the skies,
Would look with vengeance in His eye,
If I should ever dare despise
My Mother'

And oft she saw the closet door, and longed
to look inside.
At last she could no more refrain, and turned
the little key,
And looked within, and fainted straight the
horrid sight to see;
For there upon the floor was blood, and on
the walls were wives,
For Bluebeard first had married them, then
cut their throats with knives.

And this poor wife, distracted, picked the key
up from the floor,
All stained with blood; and with much fear
she shut and locked the door.
She tried in vain to clean the key and wash
the stain away
With sand and soap,—it was no use. Bluebeard came back that day;
At once he asked her for the key,—he saw
the bloody stain,—

Walter Crane *Centre Pages* from 'Bluebeard' 1875, wood-engraving.
Hornby Library, Liverpool City Libraries

Such books might be seen as a shrewd investment for the future for the doting parent/book purchaser!

The world beyond the safe haven of the nursery, the house and garden, is only lightly sketched in by Crane. Working-class or labouring people inevitably appear in the stories in the form of servants (ill p36). The Toy Books were produced before Crane's conversion to Socialism in the mid-1880s and it is hard to find any interest in social equality or democracy in his early work. Servants were a fact of everyday life for all but the poorest middle-class people. They were a continual presence around the home and particularly in the labour-generating vicinity of children. Servants in Crane's art are frequently indistinguishable from one another, or appear much smaller, and less important than the protagonists in the story who are, of course, upper class. In *The Frog Prince* 1874 (A18, ill p36), the scene of the proud Princess at table with the frog sharing her plate, is enlivened by two servants laughing at her dismay. The black servant in a turban is caricatured with

rolling eyes and huge grin, rather like lamp-holding statues of negroes. The other servants appear coarse in features when compared to the Grecian-looking King and Princess. The 'science' of physiognomy, which was at the height of its popularity in the mid-Victorian period, theoretically made it possible effortlessly to discriminate the features of a lady from those of a servant, and the face of a good person from that of a bad. Artists were prone to use physiognomic stereotypes to point out the differences in social and financial position as 'natural' or innate and unalterable.[6] Unsurprisingly, Crane's Toy Books always have clear divisions between the faces and expressions of the lower orders and their social superiors. *The Frog Prince* is deeply concerned with issues of rank and place – the text, probably by Crane, uses words which overtly refer to these questions. The frog requests that he be allowed to sleep in the princess' little bed as a reward for rescuing her golden ball. She thinks he is 'silly', 'let him remain in the water with his equals; he cannot mix

Walter Crane *Centre Pages from 'The Frog Prince'* (A18)

in society'. It is the Princess's father who insists that she honour her bargain with the frog, by allowing him on the table and into her bed. Curiously Crane does not chose the common means of transformation, the kiss, but substitutes a violent one – she throws the frog against the wall and releases him from the spell (ill p37). In the end she is rewarded for her snobbery and violence by marrying a Prince, who is after all her social and aesthetic equal.

Crane's books show a typical Aesthetic movement obsession with the redemptive powers of beauty and good design. This is not incompatible with his urge to inculcate moral and ethical values in his young readers. He felt that good taste was vital to the formation of a sensitive and good personality, and advocated that the child's environment be dedicated to this end. The moral line of Crane's books was not directly Christian – he had himself apostatised around 1864/5 – but they contained nothing which would offend the average middle-class, church-going, upwardly mobile Victorian parent. The books were designed to appeal to the parents as much as their offspring, by admitting them to Crane's own circle of perfect, but advanced aesthetic design. The success of Crane's children's books was rooted in their combination of a number of elements: their exquisite drawing and lavish use of colour; their evocation of glamorous and pleasing fantasies of both the past and the present, and their careful shaping of the mind and imagination of the middle-class Victorian child.

Notes

1   Roy Strong, *And when did you last see your father?* 1978 p153
2   Marian Orr, *Regency Themes in late Victorian Painting* unpub M Phil Thesis University of London, Courtauld Institute of Art 1982 p3
3   H M Lloyd, *England in the Eighteen-Eighties* 1968 pp52-3
4   The text was by Lucy Crane, the artist's sister and refers to a Crane family trip to see the Great Exhibition in 1851.
5   Crane, *Bases* p231
6   Mary C Cowling, 'The artist as anthropologist in mid-Victorian England: Frith's Derby Day, the Railway Station, and the new science of mankind' *Art History* Vol 6 No 4 pp462-78

Walter Crane *Page from 'The Frog Prince'* (A18)

Jennifer Harris

'Building a Fair House of Dreams': Walter Crane as a Pattern Designer

The Victorian period saw the awakening of an unprecedented public interest in surface ornament and house decoration, and the theoretical and popular literature of the age was flooded with lively argument about propriety in ornamental design. Many influential designers published books and articles on the subject, notably William Morris, Christopher Dresser, Lewis F Day and Walter Crane, and the debate was given regular public airing in the pages of specialist magazines such as *The Builder* and *The Magazine of Art*, as well as in more popular publications like *The Ladies Realm*.

Part of the explanation for this is to be found in the view, popularised by John Ruskin and William Morris, that decoration was not a minor art, a poor relation of painting and sculpture, but part of the great unity of art. In *The Two Paths, Being Lectures on Art and Its Application to Decoration and Manufacture* 1859, Ruskin charged his readers to 'get rid then, at once of any idea of Decorative art being a degraded or a separate kind of art',[1] whilst in 1882, in a lecture ironically styled 'The Lesser Arts of Life', Morris urged his audience 'to agree with me in thinking that these lesser arts are really a part of the greater ones', explaining that:

'All the greater arts appeal directly to that intricate combination of intuitive perceptions, feelings, experience, and memory which is called imagination. All artists ... have these qualities superabundantly ... But we must never forget that all men who are not naturally deficient, or who have not been spoiled by defective or perverse education, have imagination in some measure ... so that they are also partakers of the greater arts.'[2]

This view became a corner-stone of the philosophy of the Arts and Crafts movement, where it was frequently contended that not only did decoration merit the attention of the artist but also that a good designer must be an artist. In the introduction to the catalogue of the first Arts and Crafts Exhibition in 1888, Walter Crane put his case for the decorative arts:

'The true root and basis of all Art lies in the handicrafts. If there is no room or chance of recognition for really artistic power and feeling in design and craftsmanship – if Art is not recognised in the humblest object and material, and felt to be as valuable

in its own way as the more highly rewarded pictorial skill – the arts cannot be in sound condition.'[3]

For Lewis F Day, however, with whom Crane maintained a highly public debate during the 1890s and early 1900s about the nature of decorative art, Crane's views on poetry in ornament exceeded what was required of a piece of two-dimensional design such as a wallpaper or printed furnishing fabric. In *Moot Points*, subtitled *Friendly Disputes upon Art and Industry between Walter Crane and Lewis F. Day*, published in 1903, Crane's response to Day's view that decorative art is more prosaic than fine art was that it all depends on the designer and the powers of his imagination. Echoing Morris, he contended that, if a pattern 'is the product of a sensitive and intelligent human being and not a machine', it should also have 'something besides in it – something human, in short, which speaks of character or individual (or racial) feeling behind it'. Unconvinced by Crane's argument, Day retorted: 'I am not sure that I want anyone's personality to call out to me from the walls and the floor of my room.'[4] Crane's personal handwriting is discernible in all of his pattern-making and, like Morris', his wallpapers in particular were sometimes criticised for being too assertive.

Wallpaper, because of its unremitting two-dimensionality, became the focus of the reforming zeal of those who campaigned for the raising of standards of British design during the middle decades of the century. It also lay at the heart of a fundamental disagreement among designers as to whether naturalistic imagery was acceptable as decoration, or whether all ornamental forms should be rendered abstractly. Flowers and foliage formed the principal motifs for surface ornament in the nineteenth century, but the treatment of natural ornament ranged from severe geometric abstraction through degrees of conventionalisation to mimetic realism (ill p39).

The group around Henry Cole, Charles Eastlake, Richard Redgrave, and A W N Pugin, which spearheaded the campaign for design reform in the years around the Great Exhibition of 1851, helped to popularise the notion that imitation of nature should be avoided. Their organ, *The Journal of Design and Manufacture* (1849–1852), is rich in

Woollams & Co *Floral Pattern* c1860, wallpaper. Whitworth Art Gallery, University of Manchester

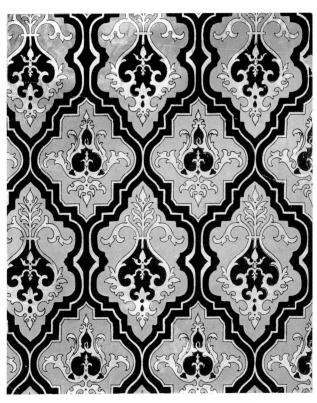

Woollams & Co *Ogival Pattern* mid-19th century, wallpaper. Whitworth Art Gallery, University of Manchester

attacks on all illusionistic and perspectival effects. Many of the small geometric patterns which the reformers endorsed such as *Ogival Pattern* (ill p39), were inspired by Near Eastern and Moorish designs featured in Owen Jones' *Grammar of Ornament* 1856, whilst others were based on Gothic forms promoted by Pugin.

Compared to the rigidly two-dimensional and formal geometric patterns of the Design Reform movement William Morris' designs appear strikingly naturalistic, though he always maintained that nature should be rendered with a degree of conventionalisation. With his great knowledge of medieval woven textiles and as a result of his own experiments with weaving, the structure of Morris' patterns tended to become more formal, a net or diaper structure replacing the informal meandering branch on which his earlier patterns were based. In his most successful designs, however, such as the *Blackthorn* wallpaper 1892 or the *Loddon* chintz 1884, Morris managed to reconcile the sense of organic growth of natural forms within a complex formal structure created by the stems of the plants depicted.

In common with most of his contemporaries Crane also held the view that some degree of conventionalisation of natural forms was essential. He presents his argument at some length in an article on 'Design' in 1893, where he makes the distinction between pictorial art (Aspect), which has as its aim the 'imitation' of nature, and the art of the designer (Adaptation), 'whose object is rather to suggest than to imitate'.[5] He illustrates his point by means of two drawings of an oak tree, one rendered pictorially, the other schematised to form a design (ill p40). From the delicate scrolling stems of *Briar Rose* 1880 to the strongly linear *Day Lily* 1897 (J24, ill p41), Crane faithfully adapted nature to design but, as with Morris, Crane's theoretical standpoint never quite overcame his emotional response to nature. He strenuously avoided forcing natural forms into purely conventional patterns so long as they could be coaxed into the form demanded by his repeats.

Where Crane as a pattern designer diverged from his fellow designers and from popularly held opinion on propriety in design was in the use which he made of animals, birds and human figures. Influenced by early Italian silk

Walter Crane *Two illustrations from 'The Magazine of Art'* 1893, wood-engravings

textiles, Morris had introduced birds and small animals into his textile designs from c1876 but, with one early exception, he eschewed them in his wallpaper. Throughout this period they were generally held to be unsuitable ornament for walls. 'The introduction of any members of the Animal Kingdom in wallpapers', declared one critic 'involving as it necessarily does, such amount of repetition, is always dangerous. Even birds, which are the least objectionable, have their difficulties'.[6] Similarly, *The Ladies Realm*, reviewing recent designs by Crane and Heywood Sumner in 1897, found them 'very fine in themselves, but I know I can never make them look well in a room', and advised her readers to, above all, 'decline nymphs, cupids or figures of any description on either friezes or wallpapers'.[7]

On the subject of animals and figures in ornamental design Crane and Lewis F Day found themselves deeply divided. Their respective viewpoints are covered by chapters in Day's *Nature in Ornament* 1892 and Crane's *Ideals in Art*, and by one of the Disputes in *Moot Points*. Whilst paying Crane the compliment of being one of the few designers who was equal to the task of 'bending the human shape to ornamental purpose'[8], Day nevertheless clung to the view that birds, beasts and human figures lent themselves most unhappily to ornamental manipulation and were unsuitable as repeating patterns. Crane, on the other hand, claimed that the use of animal and human forms in design allowed him to arrange lines and masses in a way not possible by other means and, probably more importantly, they allowed the expression of 'symbolic meaning ... fanciful allegory or playful ideas'.[9]

Crane's first essay in this figurative style was the *Woodnotes* wallpaper 1886 and frieze 1887 (J8 and J9, ill pp63 and 42), where animals and figures assume a prominent role for the first time. Crane himself referred to *Woodnotes* as marking a fresh phase in his work:

'I had introduced human shapes ... in the *Alcestis*, the *Mermaid*, and other friezes, and in all my nursery papers ... But hitherto my ambition had not tempted me to repeat the figure on so large a scale in the field. Mr Warner could tell you of his astonishment when I first showed him the drawing.'[10]

One of Crane's most dramatic and successful designs incorporating animate forms is the *Peacock Garden* wallpaper of 1889 (J13, ill p135). The way that the bird is worked into the dense foliage is a superb illustration of Crane's draughtsmanship and his ability to adapt natural forms to ornamental needs. Even Lewis F Day was sufficiently impressed to use it as an example of successful conventionalisation in an article[11] although it failed to satisfy the dictum that wallpaper should be subordinate and provide a restful background. Crane himself declared it 'out of the question to hang pictures on a wall papered with the *Peacock Garden*'.[12]

Crane's predilection for living creatures in ornamental work must owe more than a little to the fact that he regarded himself primarily as a pictorial artist. His career as a designer of wallpapers grew out of his early work as a book illustrator, and more than one critic expressed misgivings as to whether his wallpaper and textile designs were not 'better suited for picture-books than house decoration?'[13] Yet, although animals and human figures had long since ceased to be part of the repertoire of the pattern designer in Western Europe, they had played a significant role in the medieval textiles which Crane so admired.

Walter Crane *Day Lily* (J24)

Walter Crane '*Deer and Rabbits*' frieze (J9)

Like Morris, Crane often found inspiration for his designs in the art of the past, particularly in early Italian silks. Discussing the Arts and Crafts movement he noted the influence of 'the unrivalled collections at South Kensington, and the opportunities there given for the study of very choice and beautiful examples of decorative art of all kinds, especially of medieval Italy and of the earlier renascence'.[14] He must have owned or had access to a copy of Friedrich Fischbach's *Ornamente der Gewebe* (1874–8), a book of early textile patterns popular with late nineteenth-century designers, for he uses some of the plates to illustrate an essay on 'Animals in Ornament' in *Ideals in Art*. The

Walter Crane *Corona Vitae* (J15)

Sicilian Textile from Friedrich Fischbach 'Ornamente der Gewebe' 1874–8

highly stylised forms of the winged lions and confronted sphinxes in the *Corona Vitae* wallpaper 1890 (J15, ill p43) recall the heraldic treatment of animals in thirteenth-century Sicilian silks (ill p44). Crane admitted that he was influenced 'by the fancy for a textile motive somewhat after the manner of the Sicilian silk hangings, or those sumptuous brocades one sees spread behind royal seats in early pictures and woodcuts'.[15]

A guiding principle of Crane's and Morris' design theory is the notion of fitness for purpose, but the turnover or mirror repeat pattern which both took from medieval woven textiles and adapted for a time to wallpaper design is not necessarily appropriate to wall decoration. The effect is particularly evident in Morris' *Pimpernel* 1876 and Crane's *Corona Vitae* (J15). On a loom, where the design is arranged either side of vertical warp threads, mirror images are a natural effect and the highly formal structure is concealed to a degree by the drape of the tex-

tile. On a wall, however, the structure can appear too contrived.

The medieval world was only one source of inspiration for Crane. Where Morris looked also to Near Eastern art and ornament, Crane also embraced the art of the classical world and of the Renaissance, areas of interest which the two men did not share. The influence of classical art is found in his wallpaper design as early as the *Alcestis* frieze 1876 (ill p131), whilst *The Golden Age* 1887 (J11, plate III) is Raphaelesque in treatment. Straightforward copies or only slightly adapted versions of historical textile designs were a staple part of the output of several leading manufacturers towards the end of the century, but Crane, like Morris, believed that historical sources should serve only as a springboard for the imaginative reworking of an idea. The designer, he asserted, is not an archaeologist but:

'the builder of a fair house of dreams, who sees in nature and in the relics and examples of the art of past ages wealth of beautiful and suggestive material – material which he is only at liberty to use on the condition of making it his own'.[16]

Crane shared with Morris a romantic conception of pattern-making which held that ornament should possess some 'meaning' beyond itself. 'You may be sure', wrote Morris, 'that any decoration is futile, and has fallen into at least the first stage of degradation, when it does not remind you of something beyond itself, of something of which it is but a visible symbol'.[17] Meaningful ornament had become a fashionable catch-phrase by 1900, so much so that Lewis F Day mounted a defence of its opposite, dubbed 'mere ornament'.[18] It is Crane's notion of poetic ornament which, one senses from the pages of *Moot Points*, particularly irritated the more phlegmatic Day, driven at one stage to demand: 'Who wants poetry in a carpet or "joy" in a wallpaper?'[19]

Crane certainly went much further than his contemporaries in giving meaning to a decorative scheme. As an admirer of the heraldic devices which formed such an important aspect of ornamental design in the Middle Ages, Crane sought areas for the decorative use of emblems. The hangings *The National Arms of England, Scotland and Ireland* c1902 (H8, ill p45) and *England and France* 1908 (H10, plate II) are good examples of the outcome. Crane's decorative work is rich in symbolic meaning, and several of his wallpaper designs, *La Margarete* 1876 (J1), *Corona Vitae* 1890 (J15) and the *Trio* pilaster decoration 1893, for example, were advertised by Jeffrey & Co with long iconographic explanations written by Crane.

Walter Crane *The National Arms of England, Scotland and Ireland* (H8)

The subject of *La Margarete* (J1, ill p131) is literary, the theme of wifely virtue as interpreted by Chaucer in his *Legend of Good Women*. The central figure in the frieze is Alcestis, the virtuous wife of Admetus, King of Thessaly, who went to her death in her husband's stead. She is accompanied by the allegorical attributes of the ideal wife: Diligence, Order, Providence and Hospitality, who appear as caryatids. The marguerite daisy used in the filling symbolises Innocence, and the lily and dove in the dado Purity. The text below the figures on the frieze was taken from Chaucer's *The Flower and the Leaf*, as is the line 'Si douce est la Margarete' repeated as part of the filling paper. Inscriptions had often been applied to Gothic Revival furniture, in imitation of the medieval fashion, but Crane broke new ground in using them on wallpapers.

Because of its attempt to convey symbolic meaning, Madsen described Crane's design work as 'eloquent'.[20] The epithet would have pleased him since he believed that decorative art in its highest forms could be regarded as poetry, and that 'In the region of poetic design symbolism must always hold its place'.[21]

Notes

1   John Ruskin, *The Works* ed by E T Cook and A D O Wedderburn 1902–12 Vol 16 p320
2   William Morris, *The Collected Works* Vol XXII pp235–6
3   Spencer p101
4   Crane, *Moot Points* p79
5   *The Magazine of Art* 1893 p79
6   *The Building News* 1872 p291
7   *The Ladies Realm* 1897 p616
8   Lewis F Day, *Nature in Ornament* 1892 p193
9   Crane, *Moot Points* p86
10   *Studio*, 1894–5 p78
11   *The Art Journal* 1901 p18
12   *Studio*, 1894–5 p78
13   *The Studio* 1893 pp24-5
14   Crane, *Ideals* p16
15   *Studio*, 1894–5 p79
16   *The Magazine of Art* 1893 p136
17   William Morris, *The Collected Works* Vol XXII p179
18   *The Art Journal* 1901 pp18–22
19   Crane, *Moot Points* p77
20   Tschudi Madsen, *Sources of Art Nouveau* 1956 p260
21   Crane, *Bases* p258

Joanna Banham

Walter Crane and the Decoration of the Artistic Interior

In 1891, the conservative news-sheet *Truth* published an anonymous article on Walter Crane which opened with a long and disparaging description of the artist's many different skills. 'One thing is certain', the author proclaimed, 'Mr Walter Crane, AWRS, is certainly a very versatile gentleman. The difficult thing would be to say what this aesthetic "Admirable Crighton" cannot do. He apparently designs wallpapers with as much facility as he writes poetry; he paints pictures and delivers socialistic lectures with equal readiness; he writes essays and models in gesso with the same dexterity; brass and copper repoussé work and the illustration of books he tackles with similar avidity; a mosaic pavement or a needlework pattern; a frieze or a fresco; a dithyramb or a dado are all one in his eclectic line.'[1] Hostile though the tone of these remarks may have been, they nevertheless serve to underline the extraordinary range of activities with which Crane became involved. Even at a time when the more rigid divisions between the fine and decorative arts were breaking down, his career as a painter, designer and decorator was unusually diverse and full. Today, however, he is primarily remembered as an illustrator of children's books and his work as an interior decorator, in particular, is comparatively little known. While not exhaustive, this essay therefore examines the extent of Crane's involvement in this field, and the influence of his interior decorations on the late Victorian home. Firstly, though, it is necessary to provide a context for his work and ideas.

The second half of the nineteenth century witnessed an enormous burgeoning of interest in the appearance and decoration of the home. Initially this interest was confined to a small group of architects and critics and focused almost exclusively upon their dissatisfaction with the design of manufactured goods. By the late 1860s, however, a concern with the appearance of the interior had become more widespread and the mid-century concentration upon design reform had been overtaken by an emphasis upon the need for art within the home. This idea was first explored by artist-designers such as Morris, Godwin and Burne-Jones whose 'Art' furnishings and decorations represented the practical means by which beauty

could be brought into the domestic interior. The impact of their work was somewhat limited though, and it was not until writers like the Reverend W J Loftie and Mrs M E Haweis publicised the concept of 'art at home' in books and magazines that it became in any sense influential or well known. These authorities stressed not only the enjoyment to be had from artistic interiors but also the morally improving potential of these rooms and such was the popularity of their ideas that by the late 1880s the 'Home Beautiful', as it was known, had become an ideal to which almost every person of taste and education aspired.

Crane's contribution to this ideal was threefold. As an artist he devised decorative schemes for private homes; as a designer he was involved in the manufacture of goods like wallpaper, textiles and tiles; and finally, as a critic and educator he wrote and lectured extensively on the decoration and furnishing of the home.

The first signs of his interest in interior design appear in the Toy Books which, from c1870, began to include highly elaborated settings complete with 'Art' fireplaces, tables and chairs. His enthusiasm for this subject had, however, started at a much earlier age. As a child he had made regular trips to the South Kensington Museum, a place that he described as 'instrumental in preparing the way for that keen interest in the arts and crafts of design which was in later years to absorb so much of my time and energy'.[2] Shortly afterwards he discovered the work of Pugin, J P Seddon, Morris, Burne-Jones and Philip Webb at the International Exhibition of 1862. Morris was to play an especially important role in the formation of his ideas. The two did not meet until 1871, but prior to that time Crane was well aware of Morris & Co's work at Queen's Square and the older artist's mission 'to revive a sense of beauty in household decoration [and] to restore the dignity of art to ordinary household decoration'[3] was one that Crane later adopted as his own. In the meantime he was also reading material like C L Eastlake's *Hints on Household Taste* 1868 and by the end of the 1860s he had become thoroughly conversant with current ideas on decoration and design. Not surprisingly, therefore, his drawings of this period reflect the influence of the more

Walter Crane Frontispiece to Clarence Cook 'The House Beautiful':
'My Lady's Chamber', 1878, wood-engraving

fashionable and artistic styles. 1, 2, *Buckle My Shoe* 1869 (A10), for instance, shows an Aesthetic interior complete with Japanese screen and fans, while in his frontispiece to *The House Beautiful* 1878 (ill p48), objects like the eighteenth-century cupboards, blue and white china, Oriental fans, rug and ginger jars, and Morris & Co chair, typify the taste of the Queen Anne school of design.

These illustrations were much admired by architects and artists. They were also instrumental in promoting the taste for new and progressive styles in many middle- and upper-middle class homes (ill p120). However, of more immediate concern to Crane was the fact that they brought him commissions for decorative work. The first of these came in 1873 when he was asked to paint a frieze for J de Murrietta's house at 11 Palace Gardens (G2). In 1878 he received a similar commission for the boudoir of Mrs Eustace Smith's home at 52 Prince's Gate, where he executed a frieze of 'white cockatoos with lemon and orange crests on a gold ground, connected by fanciful scroll-work in bronze, green and red'.[4] Crane was evidently quite enthusiastic about this work, ranking decorative painting second only to fresco and mural painting as 'one of the pleasantest ways of treating interior walls'.[5] Nevertheless, his involvement with the medium was small and apart from designs for two projects, one at Wortley Hall (G3, ill p51) and the other at Eaton Hall, neither of which came off, he received no further commissions for decorations of this sort.

Eustace Smith introduced Crane to the architect George Aitchison who subsequently provided him with commissions for mosaics. In 1877, Aitchison had begun work on the Arab Hall at Leighton House which was designed to display the owner's large collection of Middle Eastern tiles. Early in 1879 he asked Crane to design a mosaic frieze. The hall was based upon a room at the twelfth-century Moslem Palace of La Zisa and Leighton apparently sent Crane a photograph of the interior asking him to adopt a similar arrangement 'as far as the circles on the gold ground went'.[6] Leighton also instructed him to 'cleave to the Sphynx and Eagle, they are delightful', but warned 'I don't like the duck women!'[7] In spite of these constraints Crane's frieze is a highly individual affair whose peacocks, cockatoos and deer anticipate some of the motifs that he later used in wallpaper designs. Leighton, moreover, was so pleased with the results that he planned to ask Crane and Burne-Jones to carry the decoration up into the dome – a project that unfortunately fell through because of the expense.

The Arab Hall was Crane's first work in mosaic, a

Walter Crane *Page from 'The Hind in the Wood'* 1875, wood-engraving. Hornby Library, Liverpool City Libraries

medium that was apparently growing in popularity in the mid- and late nineteenth century. In 1866, *The Art Journal* had pronounced: 'It cannot be denied that a mosaic painting has valuable decorative capabilities and it offers a durable substitute for fresco now that fresco is shown to be ill-adapted to our climate',[8] and around the same time, mosaic decorations appeared in several important public buildings like the Palace of Westminster and St Paul's. The use of mosaic in a domestic context though, was more controversial. L S Baldry, the author of *Modern Mural Decoration*, thought its richness of colour and decorative style eminently suited to the architecture and character of the English home, a view that Crane no doubt shared since he went on to design a series of mosaic panels illustrating *The Elements* for Stewart Hodgson's house at 1 South Audley Street, 1880–1.[9] However, despite the critical success of this and the Leighton House scheme, he received no other commissions for such work and one can only assume that prospective patrons were deterred by what one writer described as the high costs and 'the effect at short distances' that made the medium 'generally unsatisfactory for the covering of internal walls'.[10]

Walter Crane *Ceiling at Combe Bank from 'The Art Journal'* 1898

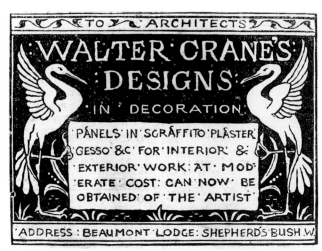

Walter Crane *Advertisement from 'Building and Engineering Times'* nd. Royal Borough of Kensington and Chelsea Library and Arts Service

Gesso and plaster work, by contrast, proved more popular and Crane's contribution was accordingly more substantial in these spheres. Not only did he execute four major schemes using these materials – Combe Bank, 1 Holland Park, Clare Lawn and Paddockhurst – but he also played a decisive role in the revival of gesso, in particular, as a decorative medium (see ill p50).

Gesso, a mixture of plaster of Paris and size, was traditionally used by sculptors for making casts. From the Middle Ages onwards it was also employed in the decoration of furniture when it was discovered that it made an excellent medium for the carving and gilding of ornament. By the nineteenth century, however, it had long fallen into disuse and by the time that Crane discovered the medium, gesso had all but disappeared. Its appeal lay in the comparative ease with which it could be used. The plaster mixture was applied in layers with a brush in a manner much more akin to painting than to modelling

and it was thus ideally suited to an artist who had little interest in, or experience of, three-dimensional work. It was also an extremely versatile medium and, having tried it first in 1874–5,[11] he went on to use it in a number of different projects, the most spectacular of which were the saloon at Combe Bank 1879–81 and the dining-room at 1 Holland Park 1881.

Combe Bank and Holland Park represent Crane's most complete interior decorations to date where, instead of simply supplying a mosaic or a painted frieze, he took charge of the entire decorative scheme. Both, moreover, also include elaborate and quite complex designs. At Combe Bank (ill p50) his gesso ceiling contains central panels depicting the Sun, the Seasons and the Signs of the Zodiac with, in the side panels, the Hours and Times of Day, and at the ends of the room, large panels illustrating the Planets. In addition, Crane supplied parts of a painted frieze and decorations for the window shutters and doors. His work at 1 Holland Park was similarly extensive. The project included not only the ceiling reliefs, decorated with a vine pattern based on the *Rubaiyat of Omar Khayyam*, but also a gesso frieze illustrating scenes in *Æsop's Fables*, as well as light fittings and finger plates for the doors.[12] Stylistically, though, there is little to link the two schemes. The gesso decorations at Combe Bank were treated in a Raphaelesque mode while those at 1 Holland Park were much more contemporary and relate to certain of Crane's wallpaper and Toy Book designs. Both interiors, however,

Walter Crane *Design for Painted Ceiling at Wortley Hall:*
'Night and Day' (G3)

Walter Crane *Design for Picture Gallery, Clare Lawn* 1888, pencil, pen and ink and watercolour. Royal Borough of Kensington and Chelsea Library and Arts Service

have lacquered and gilded ceilings and richly-coloured dark walls hung with imitation and antique leathers. Given the light and simple style of decorations that had appeared only a few years earlier in his pictorial work this ornateness is surprising. Crane himself explained the discrepancy on the grounds that 'these were by no means cottage interiors'[13] and therefore merited a different treatment and effect.

He proved similarly responsive to the requirements of the setting in his choice of subject-matter for these and later schemes. At Clare Lawn 1888–90, for example, the themes were carefully selected to complement the functions of each room. Thus the picture gallery (ill p52) was decorated with a frieze 'symbolising the arts', the library with panels depicting scenes 'suggestive of the history of books and learning'[14] and the drawing-room (ill p53) with decorations illustrating men and women in evening dress, dancing, playing the piano and conversing. Sometimes, of course, it was the patron, not Crane, who determined the choice of theme. At Paddockhurst 1896–7

Sir Weetman Pearson, a railway magnate, requested a plaster frieze for his dining-room that would relate to 'the source of his wealth'[15] and include a personification of the Navvy. Crane's response was to design 'a sort of playful symbolic history of locomotion and transport, from the earliest period to the present time' (ill p53).[16] It was a particularly imaginative interpretation of the patron's needs that managed to represent not only every form of transport from the ox-waggon to the railway and motor-car but also a portrait of Lady Pearson's silver model bicycle!

Paddockhurst represents the last of Crane's large-scale decorative schemes and this therefore seems a useful point at which to examine the extent and the influence of his involvement in this field. Numerically, the interior decorations comprised a comparatively small part of his œuvre, and although gesso and plaster schemes like Combe Bank took two years to complete, he was by no means constantly or regularly employed in this work. However, the influence of these projects was not dependent upon the numbers involved, for all were well-publicised in pro-

Top
Walter Crane *Design for Drawing Room, Clare Lawn* 1888, pencil, pen and ink and watercolour. Royal Borough of Kensington and Chelsea Library and Arts Service

Bottom
Walter Crane *Design for part of the frieze 'The Progress of Locomotion' for Paddockhurst* 1882, pen and ink, gouache and watercolour. Royal Borough of Kensington and Chelsea Library and Arts Service

fessional journals and magazines. His work at 1 Holland Park was particularly well known (ill p55). The house was owned by Alexander Ionides, a notable patron of the arts who employed Morris, Webb and Thomas Jeckyll as well as Crane to decorate the interior. It came to be regarded as a showpiece for their talents and was upheld as an outstanding example of 'Artistic' taste. One critic proclaimed it to be 'An Epoch-Making House'[17] while another, Lewis F Day, described it as 'full of beautiful things, an ideal interior in its way'.[18] Nevertheless, Day goes on to point out that:

'it is far from fulfilling Mr Morris's ideal of "Art for the People, by the People" and it is a strange inconsistency in the workings of fate that he, and some of those who think with him, should be so largely engaged in an art which essentially and must always be for the very few who have the taste to appreciate it, and the purse to pay for it'.[19]

Day's comments are highly significant in the context of Crane's decorative schemes. Theoretically, at least, the 'Home Beautiful' was an ideal avaliable to all, irrespective

of their wealth or breeding. 'Money is not what we most require', wrote the Reverend Loftie in 1876; 'a pleasant and lovely home need not be expensive'.[20] In practice, though, money was exactly the ingredient required, for interiors like Holland Park, or indeed Combe Bank and Clare Lawn, were extremely costly to design and install. The dilemma facing Crane who, like Morris, was committed to the principle of art in every home, was therefore how to provide an 'Artistic' interior at a price that more people could afford. Clearly the solution to this problem did not lie in simply executing more private decorative schemes. It was only through working with manufacturers that Crane could hope to reach a wider and less privileged clientele and it was therefore potentially as a designer of wallpapers that Crane's greatest contribution to the 'Artistic' interior might be made. The history and production of these is discussed elsewhere, so the following remarks will be confined to a discussion of their use and popularity within the home.

Firstly, how exactly were his wallpapers used? Crane

Walter Crane 'The Spirit of Electricity', part of the plaster frieze 'The Progress of Locomotion' for Paddockhurst from 'The Art Journal' 1898

himself had quite decided views on this subject, many of which were shared by other commentators on interior design. The dictum that wallpapers should be chosen firstly with regard to the size, aspect and function of the room, for instance, was fairly uncontroversial at the time, as was the view that skirtings and dados, being subject to more wear and tear, should be kept darker than the other areas of the wall, and fillings should be plain when pictures were being used.[21] However, his remarks on the use and arrangement of the frieze-filling-dado were more innovative and unusual. The original idea for this scheme had appeared in Eastlake's *Hints on Household Taste*, but by the late 1870s the division of the wall into three horizontal sections was standard practice in most fashionable homes. Crane's wallpaper designs initially conformed to this arrangement with examples like *La Margarete* 1876 filling (J1) accompanied by a co-ordinating dado and frieze (ill p131), but c1886 he began to pioneer the division of the wall into two parts instead of three. In a lecture on applied

design he remarked: 'It is usual to accompany the field of the wallpaper with a special frieze and a dado making a complete wall decoration ... Although I have made many designs for both, I have come to the conclusion that most rooms look best with the main pattern of the field, carried from the skirting to the frieze'.[22] This arrangement, which can be seen in a contemporary photograph of the Hotel Metropole (ill p56), had become almost universal by the last decade of the nineteenth century and Crane can therefore be said to have played an important part in promoting its acceptance and popularity.

As well as offering general advice on the decoration and appearance of the home, Crane also recommended using certain of his wallpapers in particular rooms. The *Lily* 1901 for instance, he described as 'useful in halls and passages', while the *Rose Bush* 1900 'would be appropriate for a drawing or living room'.[23] Whether consumers followed his advice is impossible to ascertain and, given the paucity of examples that survive *in situ*, it is extremely difficult to

The Interior of No 1 Holland Park from 'The Art Journal' 1898

establish exactly who did use Crane's wallpaper designs. However, what evidence there is (including fragments of a nursery paper found at Castle Howard and samples of the *Alcestis* frieze 1876 and *Briar Rose* 1880 that appear in the order books of the up-market decorating firm Cowtan & Sons)[24], would seem to point to their being bought by a moneyed and fashionable clientele. This suggestion is not altogether surprising as the majority of his designs were hand-printed and thus quite costly to buy. The result, however, was that even with his manufactured goods Crane's hopes of reaching a mass audience foundered on the issue of expense.

In fact, unlike designers such as Lewis F Day, Crane was never fully reconciled to the potential of machine production. Not only was he reluctant to compromise the artistic merits of his designs but also, as a socialist, he felt understandably ambivalent about a manufacturing process that involved the exploitation and alienation of human labour. However, although he preferred the freedom and chal-

lenge of working on private decorative schemes, these interiors did not represent Crane's ideal of what the 'Home Beautiful' should be. His own house at 13 Holland Street, for instance, conveyed none of the grandeur or opulence that characterised commissions like Combe Bank or 1 Holland Park (ill pp57 and 58).[25] It contained many examples of his work, including wallpapers, furniture and textiles, but in contrast to other artists' houses which were semi-public showrooms designed to advertise their owners' taste, status and success, it was clearly a house to be lived in: as one reviewer remarked, 'an Artist's home, not an Artist's reception-rooms'.[26] Nevertheless, even 13 Holland Street was not an accurate reflection of Crane's theoretical ideas. These are summarised in an essay on architecture, published in 1905, where he discussed the attractions of communal living and a return to small, closely-knit communities.[26] In this context the 'Home Beautiful' of Crane's dreams was not Combe Bank or 1 Holland Park made accessible to all, but a communal hall

Interior of the Metropole Hotel, Folkestone 1897

decorated with the fruits of the occupants' labour. Here handicraft would be not so much a luxury as a reflection of the unity and harmony of society. Today, this seems an impossibly Utopian ideal. To Crane, however, it represented a potent vision of what the future might bring and was an ideal of domestic life to which both rich and poor might aspire.

Notes

1   *Truth* 25 June 1891. Included in an album of press-cuttings in the National Art Library, London.
2   Crane, *Reminiscences* p43
3   Linda Parry, *William Morris Textiles* 1983 p129
4   Crane, *Reminiscences* p166
5   Crane, *Line* p131
6   Crane, *Reminiscences* p215
7   Richard and Leonie Ormond, *Lord Leighton* 1975 p100
8   'Pictorial Mosaic Decorations for the South Kensington Museum', *The Art Journal* 1866 p10
9   Crane, *Reminiscences* p217. Crane's decorations also included two mosaic lunettes in the drawing-room illustrating *Satyrs* and *Stags Drinking*. In addition, he executed plaster panels depicting the signs of the zodiac in the coffered ceiling in the stairway. A drawing for this design is in the Local Studies collection at Kensington Library.
10 Colonel R Edis, *The Decoration of Town Houses* 1881 p47
11 Crane, *Reminiscences* p156
12 Crane also designed a plaster lunette of *The Lion in Love* to go over the fireplace. *The Building News* Vol XLVI 1884 p442
13 Crane, *Ideals* p159
14 Crane, *Art Journal* p17
15 Crane, *Reminiscences* p444
16 Ibid
17 Gleeson-White, 'An Epoch-Making House' *The Studio* 1898 pp102–12
18 Lewis F Day, 'A Kensington Interior' *The Art Journal* 1893 p144
19 Ibid
20 W J Loftie, *A Plea for Art in the House* 1876 p90
21 Crane, *Ideals* p140; Crane, *Line* p228 and p230
22 Unpublished notes and text for a lecture, 'Demonstrations in Applied Design, S K M No 2'. Local Studies collection, Kensington Library, 39327.28
23 Crane, *Ideals* p166

Interior of the Dining Room, Crane's House, 13 Holland Street 1890s

24   Order books of Cowtan & Sons, Victoria and Albert Museum, E1862–
      1946. The *Alcestis* frieze was used by the Rt Hon Lord Langford, at Co
      Meath, Ireland, and the *Briar Rose* pattern was used by the Rt Hon Sir
      Richard Bagallay at 55 Queen's Gate.
25   'Mistress Walter Crane at 13 Holland Street, W.' *The Ladies Field* Undated
      article from a book of press-cuttings in the Local Studies collection,
      Kensington Library.
26   Crane, *Ideals* p115

Interior of the Living Room, Crane's House, 13 Holland Street 1890s

Christine Woods

'A Marriage of Convenience':
Walter Crane and the Wallpaper Industry

In 1885, during the course of a lecture to the Society for the Encouragement of the Fine Arts, the designer, George Haité, said that the history of the manufacture of wall-paper since the 1830s had been built on the efforts of 'gifted men', designers whose names were 'equally inter-woven' with those of wallpaper manufacturers. It was, he said, owing to their efforts that the productions of the late nineteenth century had attained such a high degree of excellence.[1] Included among those mentioned were Walter Crane and Metford Warner (of Jeffrey & Co)[2], whose working relationship lasted for over thirty years and resulted in the production of more than sixty wall-papers. In 1894 Crane wrote that, had he not first been a 'book-decorator' he might never have become a designer of wallpapers[3] and in one account of his career suggested that he had had to take up designing nursery papers in self-defence, after an unscrupulous manufac-turer had issued 'quite unauthorised' one of his Toy Books as a children's wall decoration.[4] However, he contradicts this statement elsewhere and, as the book referred to, The Baby's Opera (A22), was not published until 1877, two years after his first nursery wallpaper, it is likely that Warner's account of the beginning of their working acquaintance is more accurate.

It was, according to Warner, a conversation with the designer, B J Talbert, that led him to ask Crane to design a nursery paper. 'I had', he said 'long desired to introduce something better than any existing ones which at that time had not gone further than Cocks, Hens and Hunting Scenes'.[5] On being asked who might be willing to design a paper using a nursery rhyme as a subject Talbert sug-gested Crane, whose Toy Books were attracting much attention. The result of their interview in 1874 was the production of The Queen of Hearts 1875 (ill p60) in the fol-lowing year and, although neither Warner nor Crane was entirely happy with the result, it marked the beginning of a long collaboration.

The reputation of Jeffrey & Co as manufacturers of high-quality wall decorations was well established by the early 1860s and had led William Morris to hand over the printing of his first wallpaper designs to the firm in 1864.

In 1865 Jeffrey's was commissioned to print the series of elaborate papers designed by Owen Jones for the Viceroy's Palace in Cairo but, aside from special commissions such as these, Jeffrey & Co, in common with the other 'paper-stainers' operating at that time, depended largely on the cutters of their printing blocks for the provision of designs.[6] The cutters also commonly styled themselves 'Pattern-drawers' and, in order to obtain business, they would frequently give a price for the block-cutting alone, 'the drawing being thrown in as a kind of bait'.[7] The main advantage of this arrangement was that the patterns were 'absolutely practical for their purpose', having been designed to facilitate ease and economy of production. In retrospect, Warner said that 'artistic feeling' had been of secondary importance and the designs, as a result, were 'generally lacking in originality'. Manufacturers who required something special purchased French patterns but the practice of buying direct from the studios concerned was probably unusual as Jeffrey & Co was considered par-ticularly 'enterprising' when two members of the firm visited Paris to choose designs in person.[8] However, spur-red on by what he considered to be unjust criticisms of manufacturers in Charles Eastlake's Hints on Household Taste 1868, Metford Warner decided to try a different approach to wallpaper production. He discussed the subject of design sources with Eastlake and the result was a range of papers designed by E W Godwin, W Burges, B J Talbert, Albert Moore, and Eastlake himself, none of whom had designed wallpaper before.

The early designs, by Godwin and Burges, were con-sidered 'rather mad'[9] and one journal reported that, notwithstanding the pleasure it felt that 'architects of some experience in decorative art should be ready to support the manufacturers with their designs and advice', there was a danger that the inexperience of such designers might render their efforts unsuitable for repeating patterns and the exigencies of industrial production.[10] However, the appearance of Crane's first nursery paper was applauded, although there were reservations about its lack of delicacy compared to his original cartoon,[11] as a result of the mechanised process by which it had been printed.

Walter Crane *The Queen of Hearts* 1875, wallpaper. The Trustees of the Victoria and Albert Museum

By 1860 technological advances had enabled the British wallpaper industry to produce 19 million rolls per annum, the bulk of which was the result of mass production by surface roller-printing machine. Most manufacturers combined machine production with traditional methods but the products of mechanisation were not universally admired and, in 1865, it was reported that:

'the conviction among all practical men, is that all the

anticipations, whether for good or evil, respecting the introduction of machinery into paperstaining are now fainter and feebler than at any period during the last 20 years'.[12]

All Crane's nursery designs were produced by surface roller machine (J7, ill p61), doubtless because hand-printed papers would have proved too expensive for such a small specialised market, but in 1903 he wrote: 'Mechanical reproduction of artistic work must ... necessarily be inferior to original handwork ... I am arguing from personal experience.'[13] Describing his output of wallpaper designs he emphasised that the nursery papers 'being uniformly produced by machine printing' were of a cheaper quality than the others, which were printed by hand.[14] There was some foundation for the criticisms of machine production. The paper used was thinner and of poorer quality than that used for hand-printing and the machine process, which enabled the application of several colours simultaneously, deposited less colour on the surface of the paper, frequently caused blurring, and resulted overall in a general loss of delicacy of line. Warner, recalling the delight with which he had hailed Crane's first cartoon, also remembered 'the pang' when he considered its reproduction by surface roller machine.[15]

However, designing for the production of the 'highest class of papers'[16] ie, those printed by hand, was not without problems either, and it may have been his early experiences with wallpaper manufacture which led Crane to pronounce that 'The designing of repeating patterns for wall surfaces is ... calculated to demand ... much ... ingenuity and invention on the part of the designer'[17] who, he said, 'must be "commercially competent", in the sense of being able to meet industrial conditions'.[18] The design, he said, had to be both 'sufficiently interesting in itself, satisfactory in repeat, without betraying untoward lines – capable of indefinite extension on a wall-surface, without fatiguing the eye'[19] and suggested that the best way to begin was by making small-scale sketches to try out the effect of the pattern. These could be multiplied and the design gradually developed in a way which would allow both the incorporation of new ideas as they occurred and the testing of the effect of a repeat. By this means, any strong 'accidental' lines which did not seem 'reasonably to belong to the constructional expression of a wall surface' could be spotted and removed. 'In mural decoration of any kind' he said, 'one should never forget the wall'.[20] Having satisfied himself with the pattern on a small scale the designer could then proceed, using tracing paper, to draw it to full size as a working drawing which could be transferred to blocks.

Walter Crane *The House That Jack Built* (J7)

Hand-printing the *Orange Tree* wallpaper at Sanderson's in 1988
(J27 ii)

All Crane's papers designed for 'general' use were hand-printed, a process carried out by means of wooden blocks onto which the design was traced and the unwanted areas cut away.[21] The insertion of copper or brass strips and/or studs enabled the printing of fine lines or dots. Blocks composed entirely of small pieces of copper were more expensive than those composed of wood alone but Warner preferred his designers to 'draw the outlines of ornament sufficiently broad to allow of its being cut [preferably] in wood or fine enough to be produced [entirely] in copper' because blocks requiring a mixture of large masses and fine lines were apt to become uneven after continuous use as the moisture of the colour made the wood swell whilst the copper remained unchanged.[22] Crane admitted that his cartoons were 'comparatively rough and sketchy' which was likely to make the block cutters' task a difficult one but he argued that, in translating the design into a more finished form 'the original conception is ... apt to lose vigour and character'.[23] Fortunately the cutters employed by Jeffrey & Co were 'among the most skilled in their craft' and were able to transfer his cartoons onto blocks without difficulty, unlike their counterparts in America, who had required a complete set of exact black and white drawings before they could begin.[24] Moreover, Metford Warner was, according to Crane, 'a man of taste and judgement, who

Walter Crane *Woodnotes* (J8)

[spared] no pains to get the proper effect of a pattern'.[25] Warner described himself as 'one who directs' rather than someone who does the 'real work'[26] and although he occasionally suggested motifs[27] or even roughed out full-sized working plans for designs[28] he allowed his designers considerable freedom. Crane, whilst believing that any meeting of 'the man of ideas' with 'the man of industry and profits' resulted in compromise,[29] had already made it plain that he must not be asked to design 'in any given style'[30] and Warner allowed him to 'take his own line of treating [the motif]'. In this way the original idea often developed beyond all recognition and Warner was sometimes presented with something entirely different from

what he had anticipated. The records do not reveal his response on these occasions although he is known to have expressed astonishment when confronted with the cartoon of *Woodnotes*.[31] But there is no evidence that any of Crane's designs were rejected as unsuitable for production. Many of them were, however, quite expensive to produce.

Most printing blocks were 21 in wide, but varied in depth. Generally manufacturers preferred to have design repeats which did not exceed a depth of 21 in because larger blocks were unwieldy and created difficulties for the printer, both as he lowered the block onto the colour blanket and as he transferred and registered it on the paper (J27, ill p62). Design repeats with a depth of 28in, 30in, or 42in required double the number of blocks and were to be avoided if possible. Crane said that he worked within a 21 in square and, in order to give the illusion of larger patterns and to disguise the repeat, he used half and full drop repeats, eg, *Peacock Garden* 1889 (J13, ill p135). However a number of his best-known designs including *Woodnotes* 1886 (J8, ill p63), *Corona Vitae* 1890 (J15, ill p43), *Cockatoo* 1891 (ill p64), *The May Tree* frieze 1896 (J23, ill p65) and *Cockatoo and Pomegranate* 1899 (J26, ill p64) had long repeats (in the case of the latter, thirty-two blocks were cut at a cost, after alterations, of £52.15.0).[32] To add to the cost almost all Crane's designs had at least six colours. Thus, the production of his wallpapers involved Jeffrey & Co in considerable capital investment and resulted in the issue of wall decorations which were beyond the pockets of all but the well-to-do.

A trade price list for January 1875 showed machine prints costing between 3d to 2s 2d per roll but, as the firm's advertising let it be known that its products were available from 'the leading decorators'[33] rather than the retail outlets which sold cheap papers and job lots,[34] it is clear that Jeffrey & Co's market was restricted to those whose decorators might purchase cheap machine prints at 9d per roll for the servants' quarters but would hang hand-printed papers at a cost of 7s 6d to 15s per roll in the drawing-room.[35] Crane's nursery papers, although printed by machine, were relatively expensive at 2s 6d per roll and would have been out of reach of even the 'working man of aesthetic tastes'[36] whose low income would have severely restricted his decorative ambitions. Likewise the hand-prints which ranged in price from 6s 6d to 21s per roll.

However, price was not the only restriction on the demand for Crane's designs. In 1900 it was reported that 'except by a very few, and those in the highest positions,

Walter Crane *Cockatoo* 1891, wallpaper. Whitworth Art Gallery, University of Manchester

Walter Crane *Cockatoo and Pomegranate* (J26)

Walter Crane is not understood. He is far too advanced for the ... upper middle class people.'[37]

Records showing the sales of Crane's wallpapers are scarce. In 1903 he remarked to Lewis F Day that the producers of his work 'nearly all complain that they can't sell it'[38] but in 1883 several of his wallpapers were included in a pattern book of Jeffrey & Co's best-selling patterns,[39] in 1900 two of the nursery papers were reissued, and in 1910 both *Woodnotes* and *Orange Tree* were issued in new colourings. *Golden Age* (J10 and J11) reappeared the following year and *Macaw* (J30) was reissued in 1918. Nevertheless, his designs were, on occasion, considered 'startling'[40] and, although he grudgingly agreed with

Lewis F Day that a 'pleasantly broken background of restful colour'[41] was sufficient for a wallpaper or carpet, more than one critic complained that his wallpapers were 'not retiring enough, they dominate the room by their richness and importance'.[42]

In 1894 Warner asked Crane to 'adopt a broader effect and severer methods' and the two new designs issued that year, *Lily and Rose* (J19, ill p66) and *Pomegranate and Teazle* (J17), required only four blocks each 'quite a moderate number' for Crane.[43] Clearly, he had been asked to 'give in to the demands of commerce' by a manufacturer who was always 'more or less controlled by the exigencies of the market'[44] and thus subject to what Crane described as

Walter Crane 'The May Tree' frieze (J23)

'the fluctuating harlequin of fashion and trade'.[45] He bemoaned the fact that even artistically-minded manufacturers 'however desirous they may be to produce artistic things' had to give in to 'trade demands'[46] and, in order to meet those demands, designs had to 'commend [themselves] to the taste of the widest public possible' whilst being 'entirely new and original'. Thus, he said, 'the only considerations likely to clip the wings of invention ... are commercial ones based upon the state of public taste',[47] which required the designer to produce 'vulgar, commercial work'.[48]

Not only did Crane refuse to 'vulgarise his taste' for a system which 'narrowed and specialised' the artists who designed for it,[49] the evidence suggests that, although he was clearly concerned to provide an opportunity for the craftsmen to exercise their creative skills, this philosophy enabled him to distance himself from the requirements of the industrial reproduction of his designs. Despite his assertion that there was a 'very wholesome and real pleasure in ... the struggle with and triumph over ... stubborn technical necessities'[50] his behaviour was in marked contrast to that of Morris who had impressed Warner with his attention to detail. Whereas Morris had not allowed anything to pass 'unless he was quite satisfied that it was right, both in colour and design',[51] Crane was content to allow the block cutters to *translate* rather than transfer his sketches onto the blocks. Moreover, he left the resolution of any problems with Warner who, 'never [seeming] at a loss', would overprint parts of a design with a wash tint, 'or some such device', which might 'prove to be the "making of the thing"'.[52] With regard to the colouring of his designs it is probable that, here again, the responsibility was largely Warner's. Jeffrey & Co had gained a reputation for good colouring long before Crane produced his first designs for the firm and it is likely that these colour schemes were planned by Warner.[53] He it was who taught the printers to mix their colours[54] and the catalogue of the 1889 Arts and Crafts Exhibition stated that exhibits by Jeffrey & Co had been 'coloured and printed under his direction'.[55] Crane's view of the relationship between art and industry was that it was, at best, 'a mariage de convenance'.[56] It was important that the designer had 'a first-hand acquaintance with the conditions, necessities and limitations of the work for which he [was] designing'[57]

Walter Crane *Lily and Rose* (J19)

but he found any kind of compromise anathema. Indeed, only grudgingly did he allow that, 'whether rightly or wrongly', the average size of rooms had to be taken into account when the 'scale and popularity of wallpaper designs were being considered'.[58] To Crane 'the whole idea of … the mechanical reproduction of any form of art wholesale' was a mistake[59] which was, presumably, why he did not pursue his aim of producing 'beauty and utility for the adornment of simple homes' by designing a range of 'Artistic' wallpapers for machine production.[60] He conceded that 'the organised factory and the great machine industries … can be influenced by ideas of design' and went on to say that 'some manufacturers have shown themselves fully alive to the value of the co-operation of artists in this direction'.[61] Metford Warner was one such manufacturer and it is fairly safe to assume that, had he not been approached by Warner, who was sympathetic to, and involved in, the Arts and Crafts movement, and gave him almost total freedom, it is unlikely that Crane would have sustained a working relationship in the wallpaper industry. Although Crane's designs for Jeffrey & Co 'so distinctly of his own creation'[62] were displayed at a number of international and other exhibitions and won considerable acclaim and numerous awards, the majority were considered to be the work of a major decorative artist rather than that of an industrial designer.

It has been suggested that Crane's temperament did not lend itself to a machine aesthetic.[63] However, the evidence suggests that, in relation to the wallpaper industry, the mode of production and dictates of the market made little difference to his approach. In 1902, in contrast to the views expressed at the turn of the century as to Crane's work being too advanced for the public, it was suggested that his wallpaper designs 'may now already appear old-fashioned'.[64] Crane would have been scornful of this criticism: 'the only true guide of a designer', he said, 'is his own sincerity. He should contend for his own freedom, and the choice of his heart in the design of his patterns. Let him first try to please himself, or assuredly he will succeed in pleasing no one.'[65]

Notes

1 *The Building News* 20 February 1885 p227
2 Metford Warner and Jeffrey & Co are the subject of a forthcoming publication by the author.
3 *Studio*, 1894–5 p76
4 *FAS* 1891 p12
5 Metford Warner, 'Some Victorian Designers' manuscript of a talk given to the Design Club 1909. The National Art Library.
6 Metford Warner, notes for a talk given by W A S Benson at the Glasgow Exhibition 1901 E42A.
7 Frederick Aumonier, 'Wallpapers, their Manufacture and Design' paper read before the Society of Architects 1895.
8 Warner 1901 op cit
9 Ibid
10 E42A
11 JDA 1881 p20
12 E A Entwistle, *A Literary History of Wallpaper* 1960 p11
13 Crane, *Moot Points* p44
14 Studio, 1894–5 p76
15 Warner 1909 op cit
16 Metford Warner, manuscript of a talk given to The Art Workers' Guild, 4 December 1896. The National Art Library.
17 Crane, *Wallpaper Design*
18 Crane, *Moot Points* p8
19 Crane, *Wallpaper Design*
20 Ibid
21 A full account of this process is given in C Woods 'A Chip off the Old Block' *Traditional Interior Decoration* April/May 1988 pp84–95.
22 Warner 1896 op cit
23 Studio, 1894–5 p80
24 Ibid p81
25 Ibid p80
26 Warner 1896 op cit
27 Studio, 1894–5 p79
28 JDA 1930 p280
29 Crane, *Claims* p175
30 Warner 1909 op cit
31 Studio, 1894–5 p78
32 Wallpaper Log Book Jeffrey & Co c1885-1900, A Sanderson & Sons Ltd
33 JDA 1895 p74
34 Ibid pp74–78
35 JDA 1881 pp96, 108 and 119
36 E42A
37 *Journal of Gas and Sanitary Engineering* 1900 p101
38 Crane, *Moot Points* p42
39 E42A
40 E42A
41 Crane, *Moot Points* p78
42 *The Art Journal* 1901 p82
43 Studio, 1894–5 p80
44 'Of Wallpapers' in *Arts and Crafts Essays* 1889 p55
45 Crane, *Claims* p176
46 Crane, *Moot Points* p51
47 Crane, *Wallpaper Design*
48 Crane, *Moot Points* pp29–30
49 Ibid pp43 and 9
50 Crane, *Essays* p14
51 *Journal of the Society of Arts* 1898 p629
52 Studio, 1894–5 p80
53 E42A
54 JDA 1930 p281
55 A & C Catalogue 1889
56 Crane, *Moot Points* p11
57 Ibid p14
58 Crane, *Wallpaper Design*
59 Crane, *Claims* p176
60 Ibid p136
61 Crane, *Ideals* p31
62 Warner 1909 op cit
63 Spencer p122
64 Konody p116
65 Crane, *Wallpaper Design*

Plate I   Walter Crane Page from 'The Baby's Opera: a Book of Old Rhymes
with New Dresses' 1877, wood-engraving (A22)

Plate III Walter Crane *The Golden Age* 1887,
embossed leather wallpaper (J11)

OVERLEAF

Left
Plate IV Walter Crane *At Home – A Portrait* 1872,
tempera on paper (D3)

Right
Plate V Walter Crane *Italian Landscape by the Coast* c1872,
watercolour and gouache (C20)

Plate VI   Walter Crane 'Orange Tree'
wallpaper filling with 'Fruit' frieze 1902,
colour print from woodblock (J27)

Plate VII   Walter Crane *Page from 'Beauty and the Beast'* 1874,
wood-engraving (A19)

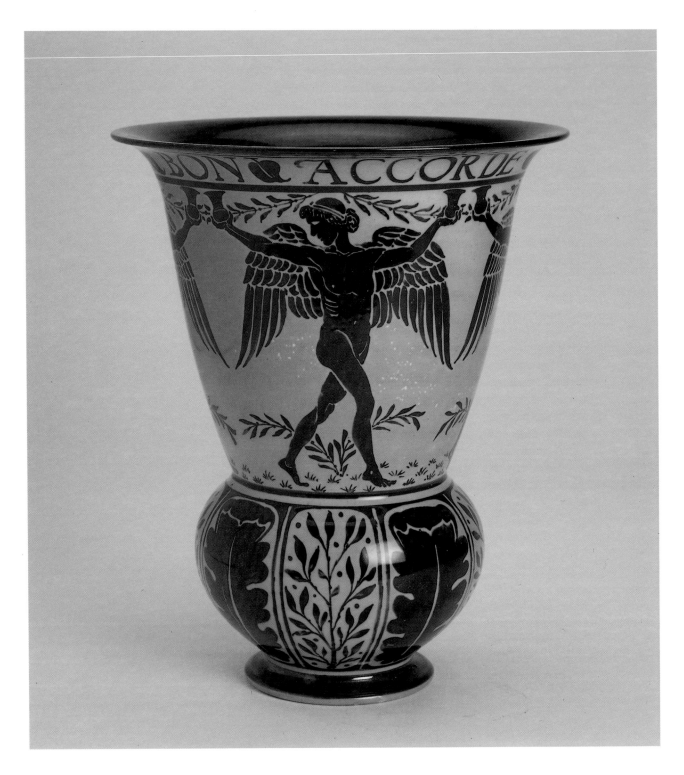

Plate IX (on front cover) Walter Crane *Page from 'Aladdin; or the
Wonderful Lamp'* 1875, wood-engraving (A20)

Plate X (on back cover) Walter Crane *Gasworkers' Trade Union
Banner* 1893, painted silk (B9)

Catalogue

Notes

Sizes are given in millimetres, height followed by width.

The date given after the title of books is the date of the first edition; the date of the copy exhibited is given after the catalogue information.

Information about previous exhibitions is given only for the period of Crane's lifetime. In the case of items produced in multiples, references to previous exhibitions indicate only that an example of the work was shown, not necessarily the particular example in the present exhibition.

A   Books and Magazines

Early illustrations and book covers

Even before the end of his apprenticeship Crane was drawing illustrations for a number of journals such as *Entertaining Things* and *The Ladies' Treasury*. The main demand was for quickly-produced representations of topical events, although this involved drawing figures in contemporary dress which Crane found difficult. He practised by making life studies and sketching at social gatherings (C5i-ii), and although he achieved a degree of competence it is difficult to see how he could have made a name for himself if he had had to repress his natural love of the imaginative as the staple work of the trade required.

Crane began designing book covers after his first meeting with Edmund Evans in 1863. These anonymous works have been difficult to trace. Isobel Spencer notes that those which have been identified, such as *The Moors and the Fens* 1863, were frequently black and white illustrations which were adapted for colour printing, in red, blue and black as in the example from the John Johnson Collection in the Bodleian Library, Oxford (ill p71). The same cover was also converted into a 'yellow back', the generic term given to the robust cheaper railway editions with their distinctive yellow enamelled paper, retailing, as here, at two shillings.

A1   Four Illustrations from Magazines   1860s

(i) *Fashionable Promenades : In Kensington Gardens*
Illustration for *London Society* 1862 p172
Wood-engraving ; engraved by
W J Linton
Image size 115 × 190 mm

(ii) *Castle of Mont Orgueil*
Illustration for *Once A Week* 1863 p713
Wood-engraving ; engraved by Messrs Swain
Image size 112 × 151 mm

(iii) *Treasure Trove*
Illustration for *Good Words* 1863 p796
Wood-engraving ; engraved by Messrs Dalziel
Image size 115 × 180 mm

A1ii

(iv) *The Legend of Limerick Bells*
Illustration for *The Month* 1864 p123
Wood-engraving; engraved by
W J Linton
Image size 170 × 92 mm
Central Reference Library, Manchester

**A2   The New Forest: its History and
its Scenery**   1863
Written by John R Wise
63 vignette illustrations drawn by Crane;
engraved by W J Linton; published by
Henry Sotheran & Co, 1883 (first edition
published by Smith, Elder & Co)
Page size 275 × 195 mm
John Rylands Library, University of
Manchester

The vignette method of illustrating gift
books was very popular at the time of
Crane's apprenticeship to W J Linton,
and, as he recalls, 'Linton himself laid
great stress upon the treatment of a
vignette and how gracefully it should
vanish into white margin at the edges'
(Crane, *Imprint* p81).

**A3   Three Designs for Book
Covers**   1866

(i) *The Whiteboy*
Pen and wash
186 × 257 mm
Inscribed with notes on the title and the
author; and from Edmund Evans: *Sir this
is the only scene from the play and book*

(ii) *The Heiress of Blackburnfoot: A Tale of Scottish
Rural Life*
Written by Miss Urquhart
Pen and ink
132 × 88 mm

(iii) *Warne's Reward*
Pen and ink and watercolour
173 × 179 mm
Inscribed: *make boy interesting and lively not
sleeping*
Anthony Crane

A4   Every Boy's Magazine   1875
Magazine cover designed by Crane
242 × 173 mm
Wood-engraving
Manchester Polytechnic Library

*Walter Crane Cover for F C Trafford 'The Moors and the Fens' 1863,
wood-engraving. John Johnson Collection, Bodleian Library,
Oxford*

A5i

A5   Three Cover Designs for 'Beeton's Humorous Books'   c1874-5

(i) *Doctor Antonio*
Gouache
168 × 136 mm

(ii) *Hood's Oddities*
Gouache
157 × 950 mm

(iii) *Hood's Whims and Oddities: The Mermaid of Margate*
Gouache and pen and ink
165 × 134 mm
Manchester City Art Galleries

Sixpenny Toy Books

Toy Books – 'toy' in the sense of 'trivial' – were inexpensive colour-printed books for children published in ever-increasing numbers from the late 1850s. Crane was one of a number of artists designing, usually anonymously, for these books issued by several rival publishers. Crane's longest-running relationship was with George Routledge and Sons, for whom, starting in 1865, he designed two or three Toy Books each year for over a decade. The books had a standard format: measuring roughly 9½ × 7½ in, they usually consisted of 8 colour-printed pages, with a colour-printed cover,

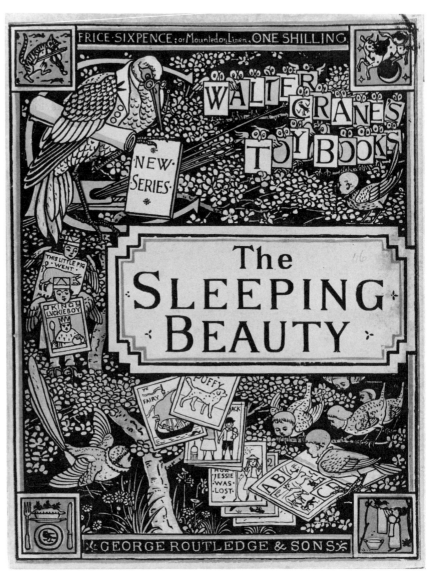

Walter Crane *Cover for Walter Crane's Toy Books: New Series* 1873, wood-engraving. Hornby Library, Liverpool City Libraries

retailing at 6d on paper, or 1s mounted on linen to help them withstand rough treatment. All of Crane's Toy Books were printed from wood-engraved blocks by Edmund Evans. Crane was the first of Routledge's designers to have his name credited on the books' covers; in 1873 the publishers began advertising 'A New Series of Walter Crane's Toy Books' with a cover specially designed by Crane (ill p72).

Unless otherwise stated, all the Toy Books

exhibited contain wood-engraved illustrations printed in colours, engraved and printed by Edmund Evans, and published by George Routledge and Sons.

A6   The 'House That Jack Built' Alphabet with Large Outline Pictures and Copies for Children to Paint   1865

Cover and 8 full-page illustrations designed by Crane; published by Ward, Lock & Co, nd
Wood-engraved illustrations; pages

printed in colours and in dark blue key blocks only
Page size 245 × 185 mm
Hornby Library, Liverpool City Libraries

Publishers were keen to exploit sales possibilities to the full by issuing Toy Books in a variety of different forms, sometimes transforming simple stories into 'ABC' or counting books by adding new texts to the plates, or, as in this case, printing the key blocks on their own to provide outline pictures for children to colour in themselves.

A7   Sing a Song of Sixpence   1866
Cover and 8 full-page illustrations designed by Crane, nd
Page size 245 × 185 mm
Whitworth Art Gallery, University of Manchester
(ill p27)

Crane and Evans worked together on the production of Toy Books for just over a decade, during the course of which both Crane's drawing style and Evans' colour printing changed and developed markedly. Initially, as here, financial restraints forced them to work with only three colours, usually black, red and blue. As well as the illustrations, Crane designed and drew all the lettering for the text of this book, in a style he described as 'more or less Gothic' (Crane, *Art Journal* p3).

A8   Annie and Jack in London   1869
Cover and 8 full-page illustrations designed by Crane, nd
Page size 245 × 185 mm
Hornby Library, Liverpool City Libraries

It was not until he had been designing Toy Books regularly for several years that Crane felt he had achieved a style of drawing sufficiently innovative to mark his work off from other contributors to Routledge's series. The main cause of this development was the influence of Japanese prints, in particular a group acquired by Crane from a naval officer. These encouraged Crane to dispense with the cross-hatching used in earlier books, such as *Sing a Song of Sixpence* (A7), and to use black for large areas of flat colour as

Now Annie and Jack were not anxious
to see
Zoological Gardens; they took them to be
A place where the animals run about wild,
And are all looking out for some stray
little child.
But on Tuesday Mamma and Papa took
them there,
And they carried some buns, which they
gave to the bear;
The bears were enclosed, and not running
about,
It was only too plain that they couldn't
get out.
And then they saw lions and tigers in cages,
Growing used to the wonders by gradual
stages;
The monkeys they liked, and the white
polar bear
(The best off of any at that time of year).

A8

well as for outlining shapes and figures. Such developments, combined with an increase in the number of colours printed, produced a marked change in the appearance of Crane's books.

A9   Book of Tracings for Book Illustrations   1869
Ink on tracing paper
Page size 282 × 232 mm
Anthony Crane

This is one of a number of volumes of

mounted tracings of Crane's illustrations and book-cover designs which are still in the possession of the Crane family. The tracings are dated and mounted in chronological order and give a unique insight into the range of work which he undertook. The exact function of the tracings is a little uncertain. Crane may have used tracings to check how a design would look when reversed, but they could equally have been used to pick out salient details from an untidy sketch. In this particular case the careful inscriptions

A11   A12

and the dates suggest that they function as a record, this being the only way to keep together an inventory of his work when the drawing on the woodblock was destroyed in the cutting process.

A10   1, 2, Buckle My Shoe   1869
Cover and 8 full-page illustrations designed by Crane, nd
Page size 245 × 185 mm
Hornby Library, Liverpool City Libraries (ill p28)

A11   The Fairy Ship   1870
Cover and 8 full-page illustrations designed by Crane, nd
Page size 245 × 185 mm
Hornby Library, Liverpool City Libraries

The illustrations for this book show the extent to which Japanese prints affected not only Crane's drawing style, but also his overall approach to composition and subject-matter. The fantasy story contains scenes shown from strikingly dramatic viewpoints, such as high above the ship's mast, or deep into its almond-filled hold.

A12   This Little Pig Went to Market   1870
Cover and 8 full-page illustrations designed by Crane, nd
Page size 245 × 185 mm
Hornby Library, Liverpool City Libraries

shown with:
(i) *Folder of Preparatory Drawings, Tracings, Proofs and Hand-Coloured Proofs*
Anthony Crane

The rather unnerving results of Crane's particular ability to combine great naturalism with fantasy are well demonstrated by these illustrations to the familiar child's finger-counting game. The drawing of the pigs is clearly the work of an artist who has spent some time drawing animals from life, but this same attention to realistic detail is then applied to their clothing, including the boots carefully tailored to fit around their divided trotters.

A13   Noah's Ark Alphabet   1872(?)
Cover and 8 full-page illustrations designed by Crane, nd
Page size 245 × 185 mm
Hornby Library, Liverpool City Libraries

The animals have much in common with the drawings which Crane executed at London Zoo while employed by Linton (C4).

A14   The Absurd ABC   1874
Cover and 8 full-page illustrations (including central double-page spread) designed by Crane, nd
Page size 245 × 185 mm
Hornby Library, Liverpool City Libraries

A13

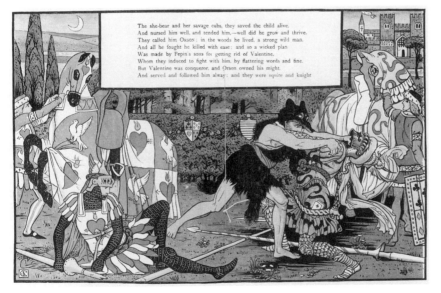

A15

A15 Valentine and Orson 1874
Cover and 8 full-page illustrations
(including central double-page spread)
designed by Crane, nd
Page size 245 × 185 mm
Manchester Polytechnic Library

One of the features of Crane's later Toy
Books was his use of the double-page
centre spread as a single unit of design,
usually marking the high point of the
story. In this case it shows the moment
when Valentine and Orson are tricked
into facing each other in combat.

A16 Jack and the Beanstalk 1875
Cover and 8 full-page illustrations
designed by Crane, nd
Page size 245 × 185 mm
Hornby Library, Liverpool City Libraries
(ill next page)

shown with:

(i) *Original Drawings for 'Jack and the Beanstalk'
in Book Form*
Watercolour, ink, wash and pencil on
four double leaves, folded
283 × 220 mm

(ii) *Seven Proofs for 'Jack and the Beanstalk' on
One Sheet*
Colour-printed wood-engravings
561 × 938 mm
Anthony Crane

Crane began to use mock-ups in book
form as part of the design process in the
mid-1870s; such an arrangement helped
him to think of the book as a decorative
unity.

Correspondence between Crane and John
Lane over the later reprints of the shilling
Toy Books suggests all the illustrations for
each book were printed on one sheet.
They were stored in this form by Evans
until the publisher required them, and
only then were the sheets cut, the letterpress added and the whole bound. If this
is the case the date at which it was sold
and the time it was bound gives no true
indication of its date of printing.

A16

A16i

A17 The Sleeping Beauty 1876
Cover and 8 full-page illustrations
(including central double-page spread)
designed by Crane, nd
Page size 245 × 185 mm
Hornby Library, Liverpool City Libraries

shown with:
Seven Studies for 'The Sleeping Beauty'

(i-iii) *Three Studies for 'The Prince Enters the
Courtyard'*
Pencil and wash
211 × 328; 218 × 328; 211 × 328 mm

(iv) *Study for 'The Prince Enters the Palace'*
Wash
213 × 163 mm

(v-vii) *Three Studies for 'The Prince Asks
Directions'*
Pencil and wash
210 × 162; 212 × 160; 210 × 160 mm
Glasgow Art Gallery and Museum

Crane used various sources for the texts of

his Toy Books. Several came from
collections of folk-tales compiled in
France during the 17th century; *The
Sleeping Beauty* 1876 for example, was taken
from one compiled by Charles Perrault.
Another favourite source was the *Arabian
Nights* compendium, introduced into
Europe during the 18th century. Crane's
sister, Lucy, composed many of the texts,
including the verse renderings of nursery
rhymes and more contemporary tales. In
spite of the brevity of the texts, Crane still
found great difficulty in incorporating
areas of type into his page designs. *The
Sleeping Beauty* was the last Toy Book Crane
designed for Routledge.

The first three of the preparatory
drawings allow us to see the evolution of
one of the most complex of the double-
page illustrations for the Toy Books. In
each case Crane picks out the main forms
in wash from a very sketchy pencil
underdrawing. The figures are clearly

fixed in the first drawing and subsequent
changes are mainly in the setting. The last
three drawings show how Crane uses free
pencil lines to evolve the design and flat
washes to block out areas equivalent to
the flat colour of the woodblock print.
Crane rather surprisingly follows
academic theory and studies the figures
first in the nude.

Shilling Toy Books

Crane records that 'The larger shilling
quarto picture books published about
1874−5−6 ... were a speculation of Mr
Evans' (Crane, *Imprint* p83). They had a
slightly different format from the
sixpenny Toy Books, with longer texts
printed on separate pages instead of in
small tablets left in the full-page
illustrations. Stylistic evidence suggests
that the texts for this series may have been
written by Crane himself; Crane now had

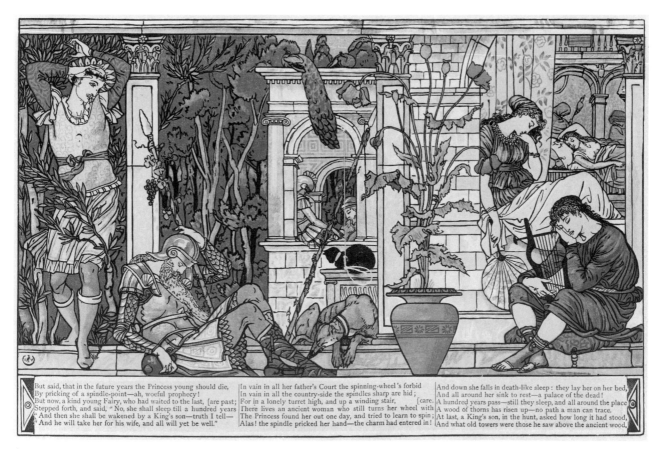

But said, that in the future years the Princess young should die,
By pricking of a spindle-point—ah, woeful prophecy!
But now, a kind young Fairy, who had waited to the last, [are past;
Stepped forth, and said, "No, she shall sleep till a hundred years
And then she shall be wakened by a King's son—truth I tell—
And he will take her for his wife, and all will yet be well."

In vain in all her father's Court the spinning-wheel's forbid
In vain in all the country-side the spindles sharp are hid;
For in a lonely turret high, and up a winding stair, [care.
There lives an ancient woman who still turns her wheel with
The Princess found her out one day, and tried to learn to spin;
Alas! the spindle pricked her hand—the charm had entered in!

And down she falls in death-like sleep: they lay her on her bed,
And all around her sink to rest—a palace of the dead!
A hundred years pass—still they sleep, and all around the place
A wood of thorns has risen up—no path a man can trace.
At last, a King's son, in the hunt, asked how long it had stood,
And what old towers were those he saw above the ancient wood,

A17

A17i

A17vii

specific ideas which he wanted to convey through the texts as well as the images. The full-page illustrations are triumphs of Evans' skill as a colour printer. Both series came to an end in 1876, although new editions continued to be produced for years after their initial publication dates, and the publishers John Lane began a series of reprints in 1895.

A18   The Frog Prince   1874
Cover and 6 full-page illustrations (including central double-page spread) designed by Crane, nd
Page size 270 × 235mm
Hornby Library, Liverpool City Libraries (ill pp36 and 37)

A19   Beauty and the Beast   1874
Cover and 6 full-page illustrations (including central double-page spread) designed by Crane, nd
Page size 270 × 235 mm
Hornby Library, Liverpool City Libraries (plate VII)

shown with:
(i-vi) *Six Preparatory Drawings for Cover and Illustrations for 'Beauty and the Beast'*
Pencil, ink and watercolour
Anthony Crane

The shilling series of Toy Books was begun after Crane's return to London from his long Italian honeymoon. The influence of Japanese prints which had shown in earlier works in the sixpenny series was now mixed with a host of other influences, some of which Crane lists as 'Uccello, Gozzoli, Crivelli, Botticelli, early Venetians, Mantegna' (Crane, *Art Journal* p4). Crane clearly revelled in this stylistic eclecticism; part of the appeal of his treatment of such stories as *Beauty and the Beast* (A19) depends on the convincingly dead-pan realism with which, in the centre double-page spread, a wild boar is shown, with a monocle in one eye, dressed with great . elegance in the costume of a 17th-century cavalier, casually seated on an early 19th-century Empire-style sofa.

One of the advantages of the use of photography in transferring the design to the woodblock for engraving was that the artist could keep his original drawings (A19i-vi). When Crane toured an exhibition around America and Europe these smaller items proved particularly saleable.

A20   Aladdin; or The Wonderful Lamp   1875
Cover and 6 full-page illustrations (including central double-page spread) designed by Crane, nd
Page size 270 × 235 mm
Hornby Library, Liverpool City Libraries (plate IX on front cover and ill p119)

Aside from the stylistic influence of Japanese prints Crane was not averse to borrowing a compositional feature as here in the opening scene which is based on Hiroshige's *Theatre District at Night*.

Later children's books

A21   Two Books by Mrs Molesworth

(i) *The Cuckoo Clock* 1877
Title page and 7 full-page illustrations designed by Crane; engraved by Messrs Swain; printed by William Clowes & Sons Ltd; published by MacMillan & Co Ltd, 1927
Line-block reproductions of wood-engraved illustrations, printed in black
Page size 190 × 140 mm

(ii) *The Rectory Children* 1889
Frontispiece, title page and 7 full-page illustrations designed by Crane; printed by R & R Clark Ltd; published by MacMillan & Co Ltd, 1916
Line-block reproductions of wood-engraved illustrations, printed in black
Page size 190 × 140 mm
John Rylands Library, University of Manchester

Crane began designing for MacMillan's in 1875. The association lasted until 1890, with Mrs Molesworth writing, and Crane illustrating, a new book every year.

A22   The Baby's Opera: a Book of Old Rhymes with New Dresses   1877
Cover, title page, frontispiece, borders, decorations and 10 full-page illustrations designed by Crane; engraved and printed by Edmund Evans; published by George Routledge & Sons, nd
Wood-engraved illustrations, printed in colours
Page size 180 × 185 mm
Hornby Library, Liverpool City Libraries (plate I)

shown with:
Four Hand-coloured Proofs for 'The Baby's Opera'

(i) *Mrs Bond*
(ii) *Ye Good King Arthur*
(iii) *How Does My Lady's Garden Grow*
(iv) *I Saw Three Ships*
Watercolour over wood-engraved key block
The Trustees of the British Museum

(v) *Hand-coloured Proof, with Edmund Evans' Annotations, for 'The Baby's Opera'*
How Does My Lady's Garden Grow
Watercolour over wood-engraved key block
Signed: E.E.
Anthony Crane

The *Baby's Opera* marks a new stage in Crane's career as a designer of children's books. The illustrations are more delicate, and are printed in lighter colours. The organisation was new too; Crane and Evans initiated the project, selling it complete to the publishers and sharing the profits. As Crane readily admitted, the book's success depended to a large extent on Evans' technical knowledge and experience. In spite of warnings from 'the trade' that no-one would pay 5s for a book with no gold on the cover, the edition of 10,000 copies sold out almost immediately.

A23   The Baby's Bouquet: a Fresh Bunch of Old Rhymes and Tunes   1878
Songs collected and arranged by Lucy Crane
Title page, frontispiece, borders, decorations and 10 full-page illustrations designed by Crane; engraved and printed

A22

by Edmund Evans; published by George
Routledge & Sons, nd
Wood-engraved illustrations, printed in
colours
Page size 180 × 185 mm
Hornby Library, Liverpool City Libraries
(ill p34)

shown with:
Eight Hand-coloured Proofs for 'The Baby's Bouquet'

(i) *Title Page*
(ii) *Frontispiece*
(iii) *The Old Man In Leather*
(iv) *Sur Le Pont d'Avignon*
(v) *The Four Presents*
(vi) *Gefunden*
(vii) *The Little Cock Sparrow*
(viii) *The North Wind And The Robin*
Watercolour over wood-engraved key
block
The Trustees of the British Museum

(ix) *Beatrice and Lionel Crane* 1877
Pencil
222 × 283 mm
Dated: Dec 21 '77
Anthony Crane

(x) *Book of Designs for 'The Baby's Bouquet'* 1877
Pencil, watercolour and pen

185 × 191 mm
The Board of Trustees of the Victoria and
Albert Museum, London

The high sales figures for *The Baby's Opera*
encouraged Crane and Evans to bring out
this companion volume in the following
year, but the 'Baby's Bucket', as Randolph
Caldecott christened it (in a letter to his
friend William Clough written in 1878),
did not repeat the earlier book's success.

The hand-coloured proofs (A23i-viii)
demonstrate Crane and Evans' working
methods, as Crane described them in a
letter written to W J Linton in 1885: 'I
always make a drawing, in black or
brown ink first, for colour book
illustrations. This is photographed and
engraved, and I colour either the original
drawing or a proof as a pattern for the
colour printer' (Fitzwilliam Museum,
MS.4-1967).

The drawing of Beatrice pushing Lionel in
a push-chair (A23ix) is the starting point
for the frontispiece for *The Baby's Bouquet*
where it is transformed by the addition of
a very fashionable nursery interior (ill
p34). There are references to the earlier
Toy Books in the tiles which decorate it.

A24 The Baby's Own Æsop: Being the Fables Condensed in Rhyme

1886
Written by William James Linton
Title page and full-page illustrations
designed by Crane; engraved and printed
by Edmund Evans; published by George
Routledge & Sons, nd
Wood-engraved illustrations, printed in
colours
Page size 180 × 185 mm
Hornby Library, Liverpool City Libraries

shown with:
(i) *Book of Designs for 'The Baby's Own Æsop'*
1886
Pencil, watercolour and ink
178 × 187 mm
The Syndics of the Fitzwilliam Museum,
Cambridge

Although issued with *The Baby's Opera* and
The Baby's Bouquet in a single volume,
Triplets, in 1899, the Baby's Own Æsop was
designed eight years after the first two, a
gap which Crane thought 'sufficient ... to
allow of certain difference in conception
and treatment both of pages and pictures'
(Crane, *Art Journal* p5). This book contains
no music; instead there are verse

treatments of Æsop's fables, written by Crane's former master, W J Linton. As Crane reports, Linton had compressed the fables 'into very succinct lines with still shorter morals, "for the use of railway travellers and others"' (Crane, *Reminiscences* p276).

Spencer dates the first edition 1887, although a letter in the Beinecke Library dated 19 November 1886, sent by Crane to Linton in America with a copy of the published work, suggests that, in line with contemporary publishing practice, the book was published in time for the previous year's Christmas market.

A25   Two 'Black Books'

(i) *Lionel's Painting Book* 1886
Book : 25 leaves
Pencil and watercolour (added by Lionel)
Page size 196 × 160 mm
Dated : Feb 1886

(ii) *Lancelot's Painting Book*
Book : 16 leaves
Pencil, watercolour and pen
Page size 204 × 163 mm
Anthony Crane
(ill p14)

The last of the Toy Books was produced when Crane's eldest child, Beatrice, was only four so that whatever educational principles they were designed to impart were derived from a second-hand experience of children (see p110). Crane began to illustrate and write books for his own children in 1879, continuing a practice which he began as a child himself of creating private books of written text with drawn and coloured illustrations. According to the preface of *Legends for Lionel* 1887, one of the two books which were published, they took the place of bedtime stories and were 'the offspring of the odd half hours of winter evenings'.

The 'black books', as they were known in the family on account of their covers, were a mixture of the educational and the entertaining. Some stories involve family members and pets, whilst in others the educational element is uppermost as his

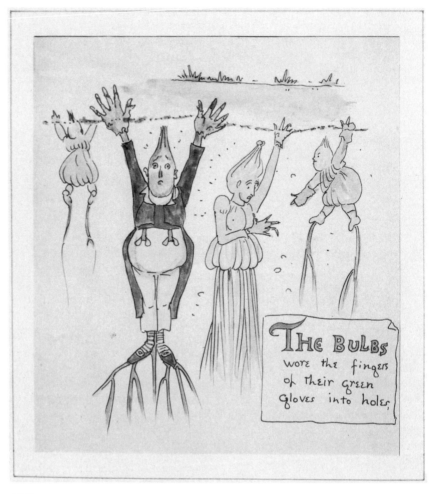

A26i

children are in turn conducted through their 'Three R's'. Others teach the first rudiments of art encouraging the children to colour the drawings or copy the simple lessons. Politics also occasionally feature ; *Lancelot's Levities* 1888-9 contains the slogan 'No Coercion'.

A26   Three Drawings from 'Black Books'

(i) *The Bulbs*
(ii) *Another Way Said the Frog*
(iii) *Pepper and Vinegar Beside*
Watercolour and ink
181 × 157 ; 200 × 160 ; 207 × 160 mm
Anthony Crane

A27   Slateandpencil-vania : Being the Adventures of Dick on a Desert Island   1885

Written by Crane
Title page and 24 full-page illustrations designed by Crane ; printed and published by Marcus Ward & Co Ltd, 1885
Lithographed illustrations, printed in colours
Page size 215 × 215 mm
Central Reference Library, Manchester

A28   Little Queen Anne & Her Majesty's Letters (Patent)   1886

Written by Crane
Title page and 23 full-page illustrations designed by Crane ; printed and published

by Marcus Ward & Co Ltd, 1886
Lithographed illustrations, printed in
colours
Page size 215 × 215 mm
Manchester Polytechnic Library
(ill pp32 and 120)

A29 Pothooks and Perseverance: or the ABC – Serpent 1886

Written by Crane
Cover, title page and 23 full-page
illustrations designed by Crane; printed
and published by Marcus Ward & Co Ltd,
1886
Lithographed illustrations, printed in
colours
Page size 215 × 215 mm
Hornby Library, Liverpool City Libraries

These three volumes (A27-A29),
published individually as well as issued
together in 1886 as *A Romance of the Three
R's*, contain whimsical stories intended
'to help little folks over the rough stones
of the road to Reading, WRiting, and
ARithmetic' (Preface to *A Romance of the
Three R's*). Crane moved to a different
publisher for these books, which are
interesting technically because they
were printed lithographically and not, as
Crane's work with Evans had been, in
colour wood-engraving. The shaded areas
are composed of tiny, regularly spaced
dots, apparently produced with the aid of
one of the manufactured tints or 'shading
mediums' developed in the late 1870s by
an American printer, Benjamin Day.
Unfortunately, even though they are
applied by hand, these tones have a very
mechanical look.

A30 Household Stories from the Collection of the Bros Grimm 1882

Translated by Lucy Crane
Full-page illustrations, headpieces,
tailpieces and initial letters designed by
Crane; engraved by Messrs Swain;
printed by R & R Clark Ltd; published by
MacMillan & Co, 1882
Wood-engraved illustrations, printed in
black
Page size 183 × 118 mm
Manchester Polytechnic Library

Although, like many trained in the older
ways of transferring a design by hand to
a wooden block for engraving, Crane
disliked the growing use of photography
for this purpose, he had to admit that the
new method did have some advantages.
It enabled him to draw the detailed
illustrations for this book about one third
larger than they would eventually appear,
the reduction in size being quickly and
easily achieved at the stage of printing the
designs onto the block. Although many
draughtsmen prided themselves in being
able, with the use of grids, to enlarge or
reduce their designs by hand, this was a
time-consuming process which
commercial pressures soon rendered
obsolete.

A31 Two Books by Nellie Dale

(i) *Steps to Reading* 1898
Title page, decorations and 7 full-page
illustrations designed by Crane; engraved
and printed by Edmund Evans; published
by J M Dent & Co, nd
Wood-engraved illustrations, printed in
colours
Page size 182 × 123 mm
(ill p30)

(ii) *The Walter Crane Infant Reader*
4 full-page illustrations and decorations
designed by Crane; printed by J S Virtue
& Co Ltd; published by J M Dent & Co,
nd
Wood-engraved illustrations, printed in
colours
Page size 182 × 122 mm
Manchester Polytechnic Library

These two books are from a series of four
guides to a new method of teaching
children to read devised by Nellie Dale.
The system was phonetic, but improved
on previous techniques by using colours
rather than a large number of diacritics
(signs to indicate variations in the
pronunciation of letters). Since they did
not affect the shape of the letters, the
colours also removed difficulties which
children might experience in moving on
to ordinary printed texts.

A32 The Child's Socialist Reader

1907
Edited by A A Watts
5 half-page illustrations, headpieces,
tailpieces, and border designed by Crane;
published by The Twentieth Century
Press, 1907
Wood-engraved illustrations, printed in
black and red
Page size 187 × 122 mm
Manchester Polytechnic Library

Various authors contributed poems,
fables, stories and essays, including short
biographies of Karl Marx and William
Morris, to this volume. The editor, A A
Watts, addressed his young readers 'As
little soldiers in the great working-class
army, fighting for JUSTICE for all human
beings, we look to you to carry the Red
Flag forward in your strong, young hands
when you reach womanhood and
manhood'.

Later book design

A33 Pan Pipes: a Book of Old Songs Newly Arranged 1882

Musical accompaniments by Theo
Marzials
Title page, frontispiece and 44 pages
designed by Crane; engraved and printed
by Edmund Evans; published by George
Routledge & Sons, 1884
Wood-engraved illustrations, printed in
colours
Page size 220 × 315 mm
Manchester Polytechnic Library
(ill pp29 and 82)

Crane described the colours in which
this book was printed as 'subdued and
reserved'. 'This', he noted, 'was supposed
to be more in character with the old-
world flavour of the songs and tunes'
such as ''Greensleeves'' and ''Barbara
Allen''' (Crane, *Art Journal* p7). The book's
format was designed to make it easily
propped up on a piano. Later Crane
recorded his dissatisfaction with the fact
that the words of the songs were printed
in 'ordinary music type which one would

A33

be hardly content with now, in that more complete search for the unity of the page we have learned of late, and which the Kelmscott Press has done so much to inform and enlighten' (Crane, *Art Journal* p7). Letters at the Houghton Library suggest that, despite the date on the frontispiece, the book was once again first published in time for the all-important Christmas market of the previous year (letter from Crane to Theo Marzials dated 31 March 1882).

A34   Flora's Feast: a Masque of Flowers   1889
Written by Crane
Cover and 40 full-page illustrations designed by Crane; published by Cassell & Co Ltd, 1889
Lithographed illustrations, printed in colours
Page size 250 × 185 mm
Whitworth Art Gallery, University of Manchester

A35   Queen Summer, or the Tourney of the Lily and the Rose   1891
Written by Crane
Cover and 40 full-page illustrations designed by Crane; published by Cassell & Co Ltd, 1891; large paper edition of 250 numbered copies
Lithographed illustrations, printed in colours
Page size 325 × 250 mm
John Rylands Library, University of Manchester

A36   A Floral Fantasy in an Old English Garden   1898
Written by Crane
Full-page illustrations designed by Crane; printed by Edmund Evans; published by Harper & Bros, 1899
Half-tone process printed illustrations, in colours
Page size 265 × 185 mm
Manchester Polytechnic Library

These are examples of a series of 'flower books' written and designed by Crane between 1888 and 1906. The earlier two books were printed in lithography, a process which Crane on the whole disliked, referring to its characteristic texture as 'mealiness'. The later book contains half-tone process prints. These have never been popular with book

A34

A38

collectors – Konody probably spoke for many when he described *A Floral Fantasy* as having 'but little of the charm of its two precursors … probably owing to the different method of reproduction employed' (Konody p65).

A37   The First of May : a Fairy Masque   1881

Written by J R Wise
52 full pages designed and drawn by Crane; engraved and printed by Goupil & Co; published by Henry Sotheran & Co, in an edition of 200 signed and numbered copies, india proofs, 1881
Photogravures, printed in grey
Page size 350 × 550 mm
John Rylands Library, University of Manchester

Most of the preparatory drawings for this book were done during a series of visits to Sherwood Forest, the setting of Wise's masque. Crane then made finished drawings for each page, including the handwritten text, in pencil; these were reproduced, slightly reduced in size, in the newly developed photogravure process by the Paris-based company, Goupil. Crane thought that photogravure 'gave the silvery delicate effect of the pencil drawings very well' (Crane, *Reminiscences* p202). Production costs, however, were prohibitive, making the issue of a large edition impractical. Instead, two limited editions were published, one lavish oblong folio edition of 200, and a smaller-format edition of 300; Crane notes with some pain that he signed all 500 copies.

A38   The Sirens Three   1886

Written by Crane
Title page and 42 full-page illustrations designed by Crane; printed by Richard Clay & Sons; published by MacMillan & Co, 1886
Wood-engraved illustrations, printed in black
Page size 277 × 218 mm
Hornby Library, Liverpool City Libraries
(ill p21)

This poem was originally published in MacMillan's *English Illustrated Magazine* 1885, each page decorated by Crane, and with the text written in 'a script of my own'. The following year MacMillan's published the poem in book form, although the publishers were clearly not impressed with Crane's typographical abilities; correspondence between Crane and MacMillan's during 1885 (Houghton Library) shows that they thought Crane's lettering was not legible; the final publication includes a typeset version of the poem as well.

A39 The Echoes of Hellas: The Tale of Troy and the Story of Orestes from Homer and Æschylus 1887

Translated, with introduction and sonnets, by Professor George C Warr MA
82 illustrations designed by Crane; published by Marcus Ward & Co Ltd, 1887
Lithographed illustrations, printed in brick red and black
Page size 355 × 270 mm
Manchester Polytechnic Library

Professor Warr's translations of selections from the *Iliad* and the *Odyssey*, and his abridgement of the *Oresteia*, had been given theatrical performances in London prior to this publication. Various artists worked on the productions: Edward Poynter designed scenery, and Frederic Leighton devised one of the *tableaux* as Crane did himself. He wrote later that the stories were 'by their very nature and associations extremely attractive to a designer in line' (Crane, *Art Journal* p9), an oblique reference to the influence of Flaxman.

A40 The Story of the Glittering Plain, or the Land of Living Men

1891
Written by William Morris
With 23 illustrations designed by Crane; typeface, borders and initial letters designed by William Morris; illustrations engraved by A & E Leverett; printed and published by the Kelmscott Press, 1894 (second edition)
Wood-engraved illustrations, printed in black; text printed in red and black
Page size 290 × 210 mm
John Rylands Library, University of Manchester

shown with:
(i-vi) *Six Woodblocks from 'The Glittering Plain'*
Engraved by A & E Leverett

A39

Average size 105 × 105 mm
The Trustees of the British Museum

(vii) *Study for 'The Arrival of the Three Travellers'*
Pen and gouache
179 × 153 mm
Glasgow Art Gallery and Museum

A41 Spenser's Faerie Queene: A Poem in Six Books with the Fragment Mutabilitie Vols I and III 1897

Edited by Thomas J Wise
Full-page illustrations, borders, headpieces, tailpieces and initial letters designed by Crane; printed by the Chiswick Press; published by George Allen in an edition of 1000, bound in 6 Vols, 1897
Wood-engraved illustrations, printed in black
Page size 268 × 210 mm
Manchester Polytechnic Library

shown with:
(i-iii) *Three Publisher's Announcements*
Wood-engraved illustrations
143 × 112 mm; 318 × 246 mm; 287 × 224 mm

Six Page Proofs

(iv) *Book 1 : The Knight of the Red Cross with Hypocrisy*
Sheet size 280 × 219 mm
(v) *Book 1 : Charity*
Sheet size 279 × 233 mm
(vi) *Book 2 : Guyon Reading*
Sheet size 276 × 227 mm
(vii) *Book 3 : 'Where when confusedly they came...'*
Sheet size 275 × 224 mm
(viii) *Book 3 : Britomart with Arthegall*
Sheet size 277 × 224 mm
(ix) *Book 3 : The Witch and Florimel*
Sheet size 276 × 230 mm
Wood-engravings
The Syndics of the Fitzwilliam Museum, Cambridge

Crane had long wanted to illustrate *The Faerie Queene*; years earlier he had tried to persuade Cassell's to let him illustrate an edition for them, but the idea was rejected on the grounds that the book would not sell. George Allen, however, had recently produced a successful new edition of Ruskin's works, and, persuaded that Ruskin's frequent references to Spenser might have created an upsurge of interest in the poet, Allen decided to issue a new edition. Crane worked on the illustrations over a three-year period, delivering his work in instalments to the publishers who issued the work in parts between 1894 and 1896, before publishing the six volumes together in 1897, in a limited edition printed on handmade paper.

A42   Three Reprints of the Toy Books   1895–7

(i) *This Little Pig His Picture Book*
(ii) *Mother Hubbard Her Picture Book*
(iii) *Cinderella's Picture Book*
Reprints of the original Toy Books, with new title pages and end-papers designed by Crane ; published by John Lane
Wood-engraved illustrations, printed in colours
Page size 325 × 245 mm
(i) Manchester Polytechnic Library
(ii-iii) Hornby Library, Liverpool City Libraries

Correspondence between Crane and the publishers John Lane survives in the

A41

Houghton Library and in the Crane family, documenting negotiations over the reprinting of Crane's Toy Books. Crane purchased the wood-engraved blocks for the sixpenny Toy Books from Routledge in 1894, and in the following year Lane began reissuing the books, both separately and in composite volumes, with a larger page size and new title pages and end-papers specially designed by Crane – 'a clean collar, so to speak' (Crane, *Westminster Budget* p22).

SARAH HYDE
GREG SMITH

B Designing for Commerce and Socialism

In a letter to the Editor of *The New Age* 1902, Crane described the degree of compromise of ideals that making a living required: 'Under Capitalism an artist often has to produce "pot-boilers" in order to live, and trusts to his leisure, or overtime, to do his best work ... Nothing in art is of any worth unless done for love' and with 'the whole force of a man's nature'. It would be interesting to know which works Crane considered to be 'pot-boilers'; in practice though there is no absolute dividing line, since many purely commercial projects threw up interesting challenges, whilst many of his later paintings, works done 'for love', have nothing new to say. The distinction is, however, clearer in the area of graphic design for here Crane worked for hire for Capitalism at the same time as he worked for free for Socialism, though he uses the same allegorical language for both. The simplest explanation for what appears to be a paradox in his behaviour was that, because of training and inclination, Crane could not drop the habit of accepting any work that came his way. His was the tradesman's approach; work was work whether it was advertising an insurance company or celebrating a May Day rally.

Working for the Cause

As the artist of Socialism, Crane used symbols intelligible to all: a female winged figure for the Angel of Freedom, a monster for Capitalism, etc. With no rivals in the field, Crane designed pamphlets, cartoons, banners, membership cards, newspapers etc, in a style which was instantly recognisable. Because he was not exclusively bound by allegiance to any individual faction, Crane's images were utilised by the socialist movement as a whole:

Anarchists and Communists, Fabians and unions. That these images genuinely struck a chord with the working-class movement is suggested by their remarkable lifespan; variations on Crane's designs were in continuous use well into the 20th century. Perhaps because they avoided social realism and talked in an elevated language of a hopeful, glorious future, they spurred on the aspirations of the Labour movement.

B1   The Anarchists of Chicago   1886
Wood-engraving
Image size 292 × 200 mm
National Museums and Galleries on Merseyside, Walker Art Gallery, Liverpool

At a Chicago workmen's meeting in favour of an eight-hour day, in June 1886, a bomb exploded in the midst of a group of police. A number of the speakers were arrested, with no proof of their involvement, and four were executed. The incident provoked widespread condemnation among English socialists, including Crane who, when he was in America, spoke out on their behalf.

B2   Alfred Linnell: A Death Song
1887
Written by William Morris
Cover designed by Crane
Wood-engraved illustration
Page size 258 × 178 mm
Manchester Polytechnic Library

A mass meeting, to condemn the deaths of the Anarchists of Chicago, was summoned in Trafalgar Square, on Sunday 13 November 1887. The gathering was met by a violent onslaught from the police, in which Alfred Linnell, a young law writer, died. The cover, designed by Crane, shows the force of Might triumphing over Right.

B3   Fabian Essays   1889
Cover designed by Crane
Wood-engraving
Page size 208 × 133 mm
The Labour Party Archives

B4   Design for 'The Triumph of Labour'   1891
Pen and ink and chinese white
Image size 387 × 933 mm
Signed with monogram; inscribed:
Designed to Commemorate the International Labour Day May 1 MDCCCXCI, Engraved by Henry Schell
Glasgow Art Gallery and Museum

This design abounds with the language of socialist allegory with the winged Angel of Freedom leading a procession of workers celebrating their fraternity. The cartoon was published in French, German and Italian, as well as English and was reprinted in *Cartoons for the Cause* (B8, ill p18).

B5   Garland for May Day   1895
Illustration for *The Clarion*
Block made by Carl Hentschel
Line-block
Image size 350 × 278 mm
National Museums and Galleries on Merseyside, Walker Art Gallery, Liverpool

B6   The Cause of Labour is the Hope of the World   1894
Illustration for *Labour Leader* Christmas Number
Wood-engraving
Image size 405 × 290 mm
The Labour Party Archives

B7   May Day 1895; First Socialist Carnival
Invitation card
Wood-engraving
Image size 122 × 270 mm
The Labour Party Archives

B8

B8

**B8   Cartoons for the Cause,
A Souvenir of the International
Socialist Workers and Trade Union
Congress**   1896
12 cartoons designed by Crane;
published by The Twentieth Century
Press
Wood-engravings
Page size 508 × 308 mm
William Morris Gallery, Walthamstow

The reprinting of some of Crane's most
important designs provided a ready
source for trade union banners, especially
the *Workers' May Pole* (ill p22) and *Solidarity
of Labour*. Crane's pictorialisation of the
labour force as simple, honest workers,
was easily copied and their repetition
produced an identity for Socialism.

**B9   Gasworkers' Trade Union
Banner**   1893
Painted silk
2680 × 2930 mm (irregular)
Painted inscription recto: *NATIONAL
UNION OF GASWORKERS AND GENERAL
LABOURERS BRISTOL DISTRICT NO 1
BRANCH*; signed and dated: H.E. Stacy
Bristol 1893.
Verso: *THE CAUSE OF LABOUR IS THE
HOPE OF THE WORLD*; *WORKERS UNITE*,
L. Stacy Bristol, after Walter Crane.
City of Bristol Museum and Art Gallery
(plate X on back cover)

**B10   Two Designs for Trade Union
Banners**

(i) *The Workers' Union, Manchester District*
Watercolour and pen and ink on tracing
paper
Image size 205 × 207 mm

(ii) *The Unity of Labour is the Hope of the World*
Watercolour and pen and ink on tracing
paper
Image size 205 × 207 mm
Anthony Crane

B11   Two Cover Designs

(i) *The Reformer's Yearbook: for the Student, the
Representative and the Social Reformer* 1901
Pen and ink and chinese white
Image size 183 × 116 mm
Signed with monogram

(ii) *Concord: the Journal of the International
Arbitration and Peace Association* 1901
Pen and ink
Image size 237 × 152 mm
Signed with monogram and *Walter Crane*
The Board of Trustees of the Victoria and
Albert Museum, London

B8

·LABOUR·S·MAY·DAY·
DEDICATED · TO · THE · WORKERS · OF · THE · WORLD

B13 Three Illustrations for 'Justice'

(i) *The Choice of Hercules Up to Date* 1902
Wood-engraving
Image size 373 × 255 mm

(ii) *A Souvenir for May Day* 1907
Wood-engraving
Image size 352 × 232 mm

(iii) *A Posy for May Day, and a Poser for Britain*
1910
Wood-engraving
Image size 370 × 234 mm
Hornby Library, Liverpool City Libraries

From 1895, Crane annually designed a
large May Day cartoon for the magazine
Justice. Many were adapted from well-
known classical prototypes, such as The
Choice of Hercules, or the image of the
Triumph. *A Posy for May Day* provides the
protagonist with a clear choice with the
dice loaded in favour of Beauty, Goodness
and Peace.

B14 The Woman Worker
Magazine cover designed by Crane
Wood-engraving
Page size 240 × 182 mm
The Labour Party Archives

B15 The Political World
Magazine cover designed by Crane
Wood-engraving
Page size 330 × 215 mm
Hornby Library, Liverpool City Libraries

**B16 Design for a Cartoon for 'The
Daily Chronicle': 'How Germany
Makes War'** 1914
Pen and wash and watercolour
Image size 275 × 190 mm
Signed with monogram
Anthony Crane

Commercial graphic designs

Crane bemoaned the fact that 'one may
find classical fable and symbolism
reduced to a mark or a poster', but he
himself was one of the prime culprits in
this respect.

These two designs offer an interesting
contrast in Crane's use of allegory
between the passive female image of
Peace, shown with dove and olive
branch, and the active male workers
shown reaping and sowing: an image of
reform taken from nature which
ironically distances the work of social
reform from the workers.

**B12 Design for a Poster for the
'Incorporated Parliamentary
Association for the Abolition of
Vivisection'**
Watercolour
Image size 550 × 382 mm
Royal Borough of Kensington and Chelsea
Library and Arts Service

B17   Design for a Christmas Card

c1878
Gouache on brown card
Image size 214 × 141 mm
Signed with monogram
Whitworth Art Gallery, University of
Manchester

This is one of a set of four Christmas cards
designed for Marcus Ward & Co, all
resolutely non-Christian in their imagery.
Crane produced a number of designs for
Christmas, Greetings and Valentine cards
for the company in the 1870s when his
brother was artistic director.

**B18   Design for a Poster for a
Pantomime: 'Tom Tom Ye Piper's
Son'**   early 1870s
Pencil, watercolour and ink
Image size 245 × 180 mm
Anthony Crane

Crane designed a number of posters for
pantomimes in the style of the Toy Book
illustrations. Given the density of the
action it is difficult to see it conveying
information, the primary function of a
poster.

B19   Five Magazine Covers

(i) *The Graphic*
Wood-engraving
Page size 330 × 250 mm

(ii) *The Art Review*
Wood-engraving
Page size 324 × 255 mm

(iii) *Atalanta*
Wood-engraving
Page size 257 × 189 mm

(iv) *The Scottish Art Review*
Wood-engraving
Page size 291 × 207 mm

(v) *The Hour Glass*
Wood-engraving
Page size 261 × 190 mm
Manchester Polytechnic Library

These covers all come from the Lewis
F Day Collection and were given to
Manchester Art College as part of the
teaching resource which Crane himself
had helped to set up. They all date from
the 1880s and 1890s.

B20

B20   Jugend   1898
Magazine cover designed by Crane
Lithograph, printed in colours
Page size 302 × 232 mm
Anthony Crane

Crane's invitation to design a cover for
the weekly magazine *Jugend* (the origin of
the German term for Art Nouveau,
Jugendstil) in 1898 was one of many
indications of his international
reputation.

**B21   Design for a Poster for 'The
Scottish Provident Institution'**   1888
Watercolour, gouache and ink
Image size 467 × 280 mm
Dated: Nov 2 1888
Anthony Crane

shown with:
(i) *Calendar for 'The Scottish Provident Institution'*
1892
Wood-engraving
Page size 299 × 233 mm
Manchester Polytechnic Library

B22

Among Crane's best-known advertisements are those which he produced in the 1880s and 1890s for insurance companies. This design is captioned *Keep The Wolf From The Door* and shows a Viking/Saxon warrior defending the family hearth. The calendar uses the unlikely image of a knight in armour rescuing a maiden.

B22   Design for a Poster for 'The Scottish Widows Fund'
Watercolour
Image size 789 × 540 mm
Royal Borough of Kensington and Chelsea Library and Arts Service
(ill previous page)

shown with:
(i) *'March' and 'August' from a Calendar for 'The Scottish Widows Fund'*
Wood-engravings
Page size 281 × 219 mm
Manchester Polytechnic Library

Crane reused the basic design of Bellerophon mastering Pegasus in a number of different advertisements for The Scottish Widows Fund. In other examples the caption *Take Time By The Forelock* is added. The artist also produced bookmarks and, as shown here, calendars.

B23   'On Liberality', Advertisement for Selfridge and Co   1909
Illustration from *The Daily Chronicle*, 19 March
Wood-engraving
Page size 622 × 410 mm
Hornby Library, Liverpool City Libraries

This is one of five poster-size cartoons which were commissioned by Selfridge's from various artists. It shows a person-ification of Abundance distributing her riches.

B24   Two Illustrations for 'Pears Christmas Annual'   1909
(i) *Health, Beauty, Economy*
Wood-engraving
Page size 371 × 253 mm

(ii) *Good Looks*
Wood-engraving
Page size 371 × 253 mm
Hornby Library, Liverpool City Libraries

B24i

Crane's adaptation of the Three Graces to fit the slogan *Health, Beauty, Economy* for a soap company, albeit one with a reputation for supporting the arts, is one of the most startling examples of the artist's willingness to compromise the allegorical language which was at the heart of his art.

B25   Calendar for 'Manchester Unity Friendly Society'   1909
Wood-engraving
Page size 498 × 351 mm
Private Collection

B26   Poster for 'Hau Champagne'
c1910
Lithograph, printed in colours
Image size 730 × 550 mm
Anthony Crane

Although Crane never stopped regretting what he called the 'vulgar commercial puffing' of the poster, he did agree that the best were among 'the most original, flourishing and vigorous type of popular art existing'.

KATE HORTON
GREG SMITH

C   Watercolours and Drawings

An art training

Looking back over his career Crane was delighted that his earliest experiences of art were through his father and that his training had had a sound practical basis. The happy memories of his apprenticeship, including long periods of assiduous self-education, conditioned his later theories of art education. The pattern of following a family tradition and serving an apprenticeship did not differ significantly from medieval practice.

Crane's father, Thomas, was an accomplished artist who made a living as a portrait painter (D6i), and painted watercolour landscapes for his own amusement. The *Reminiscences* recall a happy childhood in which Walter received every encouragement to pursue his interest in art. The family library included illustrated folios, books and illustrated magazines which he eagerly studied. Crane was also taken to exhibitions; the Great Exhibition of 1851 and the Royal Academy Exhibition of 1857, where he first saw the works of the Pre-Raphaelites, left a deep impression. There was also his father's studio where he was able to pick up the rudiments of an art training without having to suffer the oppression of theories of teaching which centred around mechanical repetition.

C1   Five Farm Animal Studies
late 1850s

(i) *Cow Lying Down*
Watercolour
187 × 270 mm

(ii) *Dog and Chickens*
Watercolour
194 × 242 mm

(iii) *Chained Dogs and Cat in a Farmyard*
Watercolour
210 × 271 mm

(iv) *Horse and Chicken Grazing*
Watercolour
190 × 277 mm

(v) *Cow and Calf*
Watercolour
210 × 280 mm
Anthony Crane

Crane's first oil painting was a study of a greyhound 1857, reflecting his early interest in the work of Landseer as well as a deep and enduring love of animals. In the late 1850s the Crane family moved house a number of times in and around London and wherever they went he sought out farms and stables in order to sketch animals.

C2   Four Drawings Made in W J Linton's Workshop

(i) *At the Back of Leather Lane*
Pencil
130 × 85 mm
Dated: Feb 16 1861
Verso: Study of a Hand

(ii) *Sleeping Apprentice*
Pencil
130 × 85 mm
Verso: Study of a Foot

(iii) *Block Cutter at Work*
Pencil and watercolour
80 × 75 mm

(iv) *Inking a Block*
Pencil, ink and watercolour
90 × 80 mm
Anthony Crane

shown with:
(v) *Walter Crane's Terms of Indenture*
Anthony Crane

Crane was in the habit of illustrating favourite poems for his own amusement and a set of these, coloured illustrations to Tennyson's *The Lady of Shalott* (now in the Houghton Library), was shown in 1858 to W J Linton, one of the leading wood-engravers of the day. Impressed by the boy's ability, Linton took him on as an apprentice to learn the 'craft of drawing on the wood, at that time necessary for those who sought a career in book illustrating' (Crane, *Reminiscences* p45). The deed of apprenticeship was signed in January 1859 and Crane began the three-year period of study which would qualify him in a respectable craft.

The *Reminiscences* include a long description of Linton's 'office'. At a period when wood-engraving was becoming increasingly mechanised and when the full apprenticeship for engravers was seven years Crane was fortunate in his employment. He was set to work copying his own drawings, transferring them to blocks for the apprentices to cut. Though much of the work was repetitive and by necessity on a small scale (later problems with large oil compositions no doubt stemmed from this), the constant practice of drawing, of defining mass and form by line, was to dictate the form and strengths of his future career.

The subjects and the small size of these drawings suggest that they were made in the workshop for copying onto blocks.

C3   Pile of Books; Pair of Boots
early 1860s
Watercolour and pencil on one cloth sample card
216 × 131 mm
Anthony Crane

Crane was in the habit of using cloth

C3

sample cards supplied by his uncle to sketch on in order to save money. These studies were made in W J Linton's workshop.

(ii) *Brahranry Bull*
Pen and ink
154 × 175 mm

(iii) *Burchell's Zebra*
Pen and ink
210 × 264 mm

(iv) *Indian Wolf*
Pen and ink
195 × 265 mm
Anthony Crane

Linton sent Crane to the Zoological Gardens to make studies for a projected work on natural history. The close study of animals was to be of lasting benefit. The simplification of forms in his later Toy Books, in which animals frequently appear, was made possible by a profound knowledge acquired through diligent sketching.

C5 (i-ii) **Two Sheets of Figure Studies** early 1860s
Pencil, pen and wash
145 × 435 ; 221 × 361 mm
Watermark : 1860
Royal Borough of Kensington and Chelsea Library and Arts Service

These sheets of informal figure studies relate to the period towards the end of his apprenticeship and after, when Crane worked for various illustrated magazines as a 'special artist' covering newsworthy events and fashionable gatherings (A1 i-iv).

C6 **Study for 'Large Composition with Figures'** 1866
Pencil, charcoal with watercolour
Verso : another study ; inscribed :
Commenced March 10 1866 Finished April 7 1866
520 × 1090 mm
Royal Borough of Kensington and Chelsea Library and Arts Service

This drawing is unique in Crane's work being a large-scale figure composition of what appears to be a scene of modern life. Crane attempts to unite a large number of figures in different poses in an exercise in composition. The laboured nature of the drawing indicates the problems which he

C4 **Four Animal Studies Made at the Zoological Gardens** c1860-1

(i) *Syrian Bear*
Pencil
196 × 239 mm

C8

had with the depiction of the human
figure. It was at this time that Crane
attended Heatherley's Art School in
Newman Street in order to study the
clothed and life model.

Portraits and family studies

Crane painted only a handful of portrait
commissions which were, without
exception, of women and children. In
many Crane paid as much attention to the
setting and it is telling that the only
passage in the *Reminiscences* which mentions
portraits enumerates the 'Morris daisy
paper on the wall, and Eastern rugs,
Chinese vases, and other accessories'
(p164). Crane was an inveterate sketcher
and not surprisingly informal studies of
his family formed the bulk of his subjects.

C7   Portrait of Mary Frances Andrews   1870
Pencil
303 × 215 mm
Signed with monogram; inscribed: M.A.;
dated: *AUG 1870*
Anthony Crane

Crane met Mary Frances Andrews in 1868
but owing to her absence abroad they
spent a long period apart. Crane consoled
himself by writing poetry: a group of
sonnets of the 'Italian Kind' about a
knight adoring his Lady. From the date on
the drawing it would appear that it was
executed during their stay in the Lake
District following their engagement.

C8   Portrait of Mrs Ingram Bywater (Sotheby)   1872
Gouache
720 × 490 mm
Signed with monogram; inscribed:
ROMA MDCCCLXXII
The Visitors of the Ashmolean Museum,
Oxford
(ill previous page)

In the *Reminiscences* Crane relates how he
and his wife spent time, while in Rome,
with a Mr and Mrs Sotheby (p132). The
couple admired Crane's portrait of his

WALTER· CRANE

AVG:15 1883

C10

wife (D3) and commissioned this work.
The result is a fine example of Crane's
ability to invest even a commissioned
portrait, which is ostensibly a record of
likeness, with symbolic meaning. The
initial study in chalk and charcoal on
blue/grey paper (Kensington Public
Library) shows the subject holding a plain
vase. The profile pose and the details of
the costume are fixed in Crane's very
precise drawing. The next stage came
from the imagination as Crane
transformed it into an allegory of Spring

by adding a Venetian glass bowl of
daffodils, two doves, a background of
'old Italian silk' and an inscription pinned
to the wall. This feature reminds one of
Rossetti not least because of the
Dantesque nature of the quotation: 'in
the sweet time when the hills bloom'. In
fact, according to Crane, it referred to the
sitter's love of decorative needlework;
her husband 'used to find Latin
inscriptions for his wife to work on
scrolls in her needlework pictures'.

C9 Woman in Capri 1872
Gouache
575 × 412 mm
Signed with monogram; inscribed and
dated: *CAPRI* 1872
Anthony Crane

C10 Self Portrait 1883
Pen and ink
278 × 212 mm
Signed with monogram; dated: *Aug 15*
1883
Anthony Crane

C11 Portrait of Mary Crane 1883
Pen and ink
282 × 213 mm
Signed with monogram; dated: *Sept 9*
1883
Anthony Crane

These two portraits were drawn on
Crane's return from Italy. The similar
format and medium indicate that they
were intended as a pair.

C12 Study of Myfannwy Crane
1889
Pencil
190 × 110 mm
Dated: *Jan 23 1889*
Anthony Crane

Crane drew his children regularly. Myfannwy was one of a number who did not
survive infancy; she died in March 1891.

C13 Study of a Baby 1880s
Gouache on brown paper
355 × 255 mm
Anthony Crane

C14 Self Portrait 1905
Lithograph
309 × 231 mm
The Syndics of the Fitzwilliam Museum,
Cambridge

Crane executed only a few etchings as
well as this single lithograph. The
intention seems to have been to distribute
copies privately, in contrast to the public
nature of the oil self portrait which he
presented to the Uffizi Gallery in Florence
in 1912.

C15 Portrait of Mary Crane in India
1906
Watercolour
238 × 175 mm
Signed with monogram
Anthony Crane

The Cranes visited India in 1906–7
where they travelled widely. Crane
described his experiences in a book, *India
Impressions* 1907. The self-financing nature
of the trip was underlined by the
exhibition held of the drawings which
he had made as illustrations.

Landscapes at home and abroad

Crane painted and drew landscapes
throughout his career, but it was only in
the latter part of the 1880s when, first at
the Grosvenor Gallery, and then after his
election to the Royal Watercolour Society
in 1888, that he regularly exhibited them.
Thereafter he usually showed the results
of the previous summer's holiday.
Ironically, these rarely rise above the level
of the competent and it was the earlier
works, more closely rooted in the
observation of nature, which were the
more successful.

Crane was always responsive to new
locations and loved travelling. This found
expression in numerous sketches jotted
down in small pocket notebooks. The
majority of the sketchbooks are in the
Houghton Library, as are a number of the
comic sketches which he made on his
travels.

**C16 Sketchbook, Compiled in
Norley, Derbyshire** 1867
27 leaves
Page exhibited: *River Scene*
Pencil and watercolour and some ink
270 × 367 mm
Anthony Crane

Crane first visited Derbyshire in the
summer of 1863 with J R Wise. The two
men had collaborated on *The New Forest*
(A2), and Wise hoped to produce a
sequel on the Peak District. Although
Wise could not take the project further,

Crane was so taken with the area around
Derwent Dale, which was then remote
and unspoilt, that he returned each
summer until 1871. Although he stayed
with friends in a congenial setting, his
main motive for returning was to record
the beauty of the varied countryside. The
detailed notes referring to landscape in a
sketchbook, dated 1866, in the Houghton
Library, suggest that, for a few years at
least, Crane harboured ambitions of
becoming a landscape watercolourist. He
noted that 'watercolour is uniformly the
best process for outdoor work' but that it
was necessary to make 'various studies of
detail' the 'shade' and 'the colour' in case
rain drove one indoors.

**C17 Vietri on the Gulf of Salerno,
from Cava dei Terreni** 1872
Watercolour and gouache
201 × 311 mm
Inscribed on back: *Walter Crane Italian Study*
1872
Whitworth Art Gallery, University of
Manchester
(ill p16)

On their honeymoon in Italy the Cranes
spent part of the summer of 1872
travelling along the Neapolitan coast,
moving inland 'to Cava dei Terreni, a
delightful spot among hills and chestnut
woods, a little inland from the sea,
commanding a view of the Gulf of
Salerno and the town of Vietri' (Crane,
Reminiscences pp146–7). Crane mentions a
vineyard in front of the 'delightful old
mansion' where they stayed and this
accords with the view in this drawing.

C18 Cava dei Terreni 1872
Watercolour and gouache
340 × 250 mm
Signed with monogram; dated: 1872;
inscribed: *CAVA DEI TERRENI*
Christopher and Jenny Newall

This scene may represent either the
garden of the monastery of SS Trinità
della Cava or the 'charming old formal
garden behind with box hedges and
pomegranate trees and hydrangeas'
(Crane, *Reminiscences* p146) behind the
pension where the Cranes stayed.

C18

C19

C19 An Italian Villa 1872
Watercolour with surface scratching
189 × 352 mm
Signed with monogram; dated: 1872
Whitworth Art Gallery, University of
Manchester

Given the climate of Italy, one might have
expected Crane to have completed his
landscape watercolours out of doors. The
discovery of a pencil study for this work
(Peter Nahum), however, suggests that
the landscape watercolours were
completed indoors from, as here, a
drawing. There is a large group of
sketches and drawings of Roman scenes
in the Gabinetti d' Estampe in Rome. The
identity of the villa remains unknown.

**C20 Italian Landscape by the
Coast** c1872
Watercolour and gouache
352 × 255 mm
Mr and Mrs R R C Parsons
(plate V)

Though this work is not signed there is
no doubt that it is by Crane, possibly

made on an excursion to Capri during his
first trip to Italy.

C21 Eight Studies Made in Italy
1872–3, 1882
(i) *Juggernaut at Sorrento*
(ii) *A Pastoral Visit*
(iii) *A New Year's Gift*
(iv) *A Satyr*
(v) *Pleasures of the Table*
(vi) *Albano – Nov 1 '82 Relief recently discovered
at Albano* (ill next page)
(vii) *Force and Fraud*
(viii) *A Fireside Discussion*
Pen and ink
Average size 60 × 100 mm
Inscribed with titles in Crane's hand
Anthony Crane

At least four of these caricatures were
produced on Crane's honeymoon and
relate to a volume inscribed *An Artist's
Honeymoon* in the Houghton Library. These
miscellaneous sheets give some idea of
Crane's love of travel and the sense of
humour that he brought to bear on the
absurdities of life.

**C22 Five Drawings from an
'Account of a Trip to Wales'** 1885
(i) *Pilgrims to St Davids*
(ii) *St DLTC*
(iii) *St Lance and a Lot of Forces* (ill next page)
(iv) *Defend the City of Sofa*
(v) *Attack on the Fort*
Watercolour and ink
Each 194 × 150 mm
Inscribed with titles in Crane's hand
Anthony Crane

The annual holiday in 1885 was to St
David's Bay in Wales where the family
spent time with Mrs Molesworth, the
authoress of children's books which
Crane illustrated, and her daughters.

**C23 Nine Studies Made on Various
Travels**
(i) *The Round Table at Winnetka*
(ii) *The Millionaire Bird*
(iii) *Pleasures of the Simple Life – A Raid of Wasps*
(iv) *The Harvest Bug and his Kinds*
(v) *Every Dog Has His Day – But Ours Has
Every Day*
(vi) *Greetings from Llangranog*

Relief recently discovered at Albano
supposed to represent a Bacchanalian procession.

C21vi

Sir Lance & a lot of forces
defend the city of Sofa.

C22iii

(vii) *Drenched Rats Weather*
(viii) *Tootles the Vampire*
(ix) *Birthday Greetings*
Pen and ink
Average size 60 × 100 mm
Inscribed with titles in Crane's hand
Anthony Crane

Four of these drawings relate to the American trip which the Crane family undertook in 1891–2, ostensibly to accompany a travelling exhibition of Crane's work, but which left Crane time to sightsee and to assess the political climate. Crane amused himself by making numerous sketches, some of which were in the form of an illustrated journal, *A Flight of Cranes* (Houghton Library).

C24   Whitby Abbey   late 1870s
Watercolour
260 × 368 mm
Christopher and Jenny Newall

Crane visited Whitby in 1875 and was delighted with the town and the view of the ruined Abbey. This may well be the *View of Whitby* exhibited at the Grosvenor Gallery in 1877.

C25   Bamborough Castle from the West   1877
Watercolour and gouache
130 × 360 mm
Signed and dated: *Aug 10/77*
Private Collection

Crane visited Bamborough (Bamburgh) on the Northumberland coast in the summer of 1877 and delighted in a thoroughly unspoilt and romantic location which, apart from providing this view, also inspired a major oil *The Laidley Worm of Spindleton Heugh* exhibited in 1881 (ill p16).

C26   Anvil Point, Swanage   1884
Watercolour
182 × 260 mm
Signed with monogram; inscribed: *Sept*
The FORBES Magazine Collection, New York

Crane visited Swanage in Dorset in 1874 and again in 1884; this watercolour is

C26

likely to date from the later trip. Even allowing for the fact that the foreground is left unfinished, the broader handling would suggest a later date and it may have been one of the three views of Swanage exhibited at the Grosvenor Gallery in 1886–7.

Works for public exhibition: classical/medieval

In the second half of the 1860s Crane was associated with a group of young artists who exhibited at the Dudley Gallery. They were united by age, the location of their studios (in the Bloomsbury area of London) and by a shared love of the work of Edward Burne-Jones. Crane wrote later of how 'The curtain had been lifted, and we had had a glimpse into a magic world of romance and pictured poetry, peopled

with ghosts of "ladies dead and lovely knights," – a twilight world of dark mysterious woodlands, haunted streams, meads of deep green starred with burning flowers, veiled in a dim and mystic light' (Crane, *Reminiscences* p84).

This description gives a good impression of a number of Crane's works of these years, including *The White Knight* of 1870 and *Ormuzd and Ahriman* of 1868–70. However, Crane was at the same time just as likely to work in a more classical vein. He was typical of a generation of artists who felt that they could take what they wanted from the past, whether it was stories, myths and legends or stylistic details. Crane's view of the past was such that a medieval romance embodied the same truths about Man as a classical myth or biblical story.

C27 The Three Paths 1869
Watercolour
457 × 305 mm
Signed with monogram; dated: 1869
The Board of Trustees of the Victoria and Albert Museum, London

This watercolour is based on an illustration to *Charmshire*, a story in *King Gab's Story Bag* published in 1869. It tells the story of the prince who was brave enough to choose the most difficult of three paths. A note in the Victoria and Albert Museum acquisition register, however, states 'Mr Crane says this is an ideal subject intended to illustrate a sonnet of his own which was never published 25.Ap.1896'.

There are three extant preparatory drawings for the work, two in the possession of Anthony Crane and a

C28

finished study of the three figures in
Kensington Public Library.

C28   A Pastoral   1872
Gouache
494 × 685 mm
Signed with monogram; inscribed:
ROMA MDCCCLXXII
Ulster Museum, Belfast

The view from Rome looking out over
the Campagna towards the Alban hills, is
enlivened by a group of rustic figures
which, taken with the title, suggest a
sense of continuity between modern
Rome and the classical past. The figures
have much in common with *Pan Pipes*
(C31). Only the gentle intrusion of
modern architecture suggests that this is

anything other than a scene from the
Golden Age.

C29   The Advent of Spring   1876
Watercolour and brown ink
149 × 105 mm
National Museums and Galleries on
Merseyside, Walker Art Gallery, Liverpool

Crane, together with Kate Greenaway and
others, was commissioned by Marcus
Ward & Co to provide designs for
Valentine cards and these were published in book form in 1876 as *The Quiver
of Love*. Crane was unhappy with the
reproduction of his drawings and this
work bears little resemblance to the
printed version. It illustrates Edmund
Spenser's *Spring* and is one of a number of

subjects which Crane took from the poet,
culminating in the illustrated edition of
his *Faerie Queene* (A41). The herald of
spring is Hermes.

C30   Study for 'Europa'   c1881
Watercolour and gouache
244 × 534 mm
Whitworth Art Gallery, University of
Manchester

This drawing illustrates the story of
Europa who was carried off into the sea
at Tyre by Jupiter in the form of a bull.
The oil for which this was a study was
formerly in the Seeger collection in
Berlin, but is now untraced. It differed in
a few details only, and in the degree of
finish, from the drawing. Another study

C29

in pencil of the bull and the figure of
Europa is in the possession of Anthony
Crane, as well as a sheet of four studies
of the bull from different angles. The
latter is likely to be associated with a clay
modello of a bull which Crane executed as
a study of the work.

**C31   Study for the Frontispiece to
the Second Edition of 'Pan Pipes'**
1884
Watercolour and pen and ink
265 × 184 mm
Signed with monogram; dated: '84
The Trustees of the British Museum
(ill next page)

In the *Bases of Design* Crane discussed the
character of the main classical deities and
their representation in art. Pan is
described as a 'mild and gentle deity …
symbolical of spontaneous nature and
simple animal existence, piping on his
reeds' (p233). Crane considered the
subject of Pan, the mythical origin of
music, as a suitable choice for the
frontispiece for the second edition of *Pan
Pipes* (A33). Perhaps because of the frankly
pagan and dark side to Pan's character
Crane felt it necessary to show him at one
remove as a relief sculpture on which the
shepherd, his innocent successor, rests.
The spare compositional structure,

composed of few simple curves, was an
important one for Crane, one which he
used to suggest a carefree, natural
existence (Crane, *Line* pp158−9).

C32   The Swan King   1895
Coloured chalk with bodycolour

C32

902 × 560 mm
Signed and dated: 1895
The FORBES Magazine Collection, New
York

Crane visited Bayreuth in 1893 and in a
long passage in the *Reminiscences* gives a

C31

detailed picture of his impressions of the three Wagner operas he saw, *Lohengrin*, *Tannhäuser* and *Parsifal* (p424). Although he thought 'the music was wonderful' the staging left him dissatisfied : 'Lohengrin did not look sufficiently romantic'. Given Wagner's use of symbolism and legend it is not surprising that Crane should have been an early admirer and that he should join a growing number of artists who illustrated Wagnerian themes. In addition to this work, inspired by *Lohengrin*, Crane also exhibited *Swan Maidens* 1894 and *The Valkyrie's Ride* 1903.

C33 (i-ii)   **Two Studies of Prometheus**   *c*1906
Gouache on blue paper
347 × 222 ; 347 × 245 mm
Anthony Crane

Crane was an ardent admirer of the poetry of Shelley. While in Rome in 1872 he visted the poet's tomb and composed a sonnet which emphasised the immortality of his ideals and their significance in the battle between Freedom and Falsehood. Crane exhibited *Prometheus Unbound*, the last of a number of themes derived from Shelley's work, in 1906. These drawings are probably not studies for the exhibited work but variations on the theme which make explicit the political meaning of the allegory. In the first scene the figure is shown bound and struggling ; in the second he acquires the cap of Liberty, has broken his chains and is shown triumphing over the imperial eagle.

C34   **Death and Commerce**
Wash and ink
215 × 165 mm
Signed with monogram
Anthony Crane

Although the subject has not been identified, the meaning is clear enough : the Capitalist is riding the same horse as Death through an industrial wasteland.

Drawing for a purpose

Paintings such as *Love's Altar* (D1) and *A Herald of Spring* (D2) and watercolours like *An Italian Villa* (C19) were the product of a careful working method in which detailed drawings from life had an important part to play. But as the artist developed his ideas about the role of the

C34

Walter Crane *Sketch for Decorations of the North Wall of the Red Cross Hall*, photographed by Emery Walker (sketch now lost)

imagination drawings began to take on a new role. In the chapter 'Of The Choice of Line' from *Line and Form* Crane recommended to 'draw simply a succession of strokes with any point upon paper, and we find that we are gradually led to repeat a particular kind of stroke, a particular degree of line, partly because it seems to be produced with more ease, and partly because it appears to have the pleasantest effect'. He even talks of a 'kind of natural selection' (p51). It is the act of drawing itself and not the careful study of nature which came to dominate Crane's approach. The rhythm of the hand, the nature of the medium and paper and the artist's memory of forms leads to the evolution of the form.

C36

C35

C35 Study for 'Alice Ayres' for the Red Cross Hall, Southwark c1889
Gouache and ink on brown paper
1114 × 731 mm
Royal Borough of Kensington and Chelsea
Library and Arts Service

In the *Reminiscences* Crane explained how the large-scale panels depicting heroic deeds of the working classes for the Red Cross Hall, Southwark (ill p23) were executed: 'I made a quarter size cartoon in pastel of the subject from my small scale sketch, and this Mrs Barrington enlarged on to the full-sized fibrous plaster panel, which was sent to her studio. I made some studies from a fireman … and the painting was started by Mrs Barrington (in oil on the plaster ground), and I added finishing touches' (p359). This study is in Crane's favoured sketching medium of gouache and wash on a thick brown paper. The scene shows a local girl, Alice Ayres, a nursery maid who rescued her master's children from a fire only to lose her own life.

C36 Study of Knights Jousting
Gouache and wash on brown paper
393 × 548 mm
Royal Borough of Kensington and Chelsea
Library and Arts Service

This spirited drawing demonstrates the sad gap between the energy and spontaneous invention of Crane's later sketches and the laboured nature of his exhibited works.

C37 Study for a Frieze for the Metropolitan Assurance Society: 'The Seven Ages of Man' 1890
Pencil and pen
130 × 347 mm
Anthony Crane

shown with:
(i-iii) *Three Studies for 'The Seven Ages of Man'*
1890
Pencil; pencil and ink; gouache on brown paper
180 × 226; 126 × 344; 365 × 555 mm
Royal Borough of Kensington and Chelsea
Library and Arts Service

These four drawings show some of the stages which Crane might have gone through while designing: a free pencil sketch, a tracing to pick out the dominant lines, and the use of pen over pencil to highlight favoured forms. The sketches in Kensington are annotated with a breakdown of costs involved in the next stage; Crane estimated £250–300 for full-size working drawings or cartoons. The project did not get beyond this stage.

GREG SMITH

D Oil and Tempera

Crane learnt the rudiments of painting in oil in his father's studio and was sufficiently proficient for a work, *The Lady of Shalott*, to have been accepted by the Royal Academy in 1862, when the artist was only seventeen (Yale Center for British Art). This, apart from *At Home* 1872 (D3), was Crane's only successful Academy submission. Crane initially showed only watercolours at the Dudley Gallery but, from the middle of the 1870s, he began to exhibit oils too. From 1877 he also showed at the annual exhibition at the Grosvenor Gallery, making his debut with *The Renascence of Venus* 1877 (D4, ill p19) which was shown alongside groups of work by Burne-Jones and Whistler. He continued to exhibit there for a decade.

In spite of initial praise for *The Renascence of Venus*, Crane's paintings never achieved the success in this country which he felt they deserved. Part of the problem lay with Crane's ambivalent attitude towards the medium. On the one hand he craved the recognition accorded to the successful painter, whilst on the other he argued for a more democratic union of the arts. In an essay 'The Relation of the Easel Picture to Decorative Art' he talked of the necessity of considering painting, not as an independent unit, but as part of a decorative scheme and called for what he described as 'a mural feeling'. This meant a 'certain flatness of treatment with choice of simple planes, and pure and low toned colours, together with a certain ornamental dignity or architectural feeling in the structure of the forms and lines of composition' (Crane, *Ideals* p267). Low-toned colours and flatness are two of the qualities which went against the grain; he also disliked the use of impasto and rich fluent brushwork, rejected for their personal intrusiveness. Not

surprisingly, Crane frequently chose tempera as the medium for his exhibited work. The revival of use of the ancient medium led to the founding of the Tempera Society 1900, of which Crane was a member and exhibitor. Of the different recipes Crane favoured the use of an egg-yolk binding agent for powder colours; he also frequently used a smooth gesso ground.

D1 Love's Altar 1870
Oil on canvas
780 × 555 mm
Signed with monogram; dated 1870
William Morris Gallery, Walthamstow
(ill p15)

shown with:
(i-ii) *Two Studies for 'Love's Altar'* 1870
Pencil; pencil and watercolour
301 × 226; 193 × 134 mm
Anthony Crane

This work was exhibited at the Old Bond Street Gallery where it attracted much adverse criticism. *The Art Journal* called it 'an irreverent parody' and commented on 'the incongruity of medieval treatment coupled with classical costume and accessories' (1870, p211). The work would have been more shocking if it had been known that the image over the altar was that of Mary Frances Andrews to whom Crane was engaged. Crane wrote a sonnet to accompany the work:
'No more I go to worship with the crowd
In Christian temples pagan now to me
                    … I have a shrine
A holiest of holies – Love's sweet home,
On whose white altar lies life's bread and
    wine
For thee, though not a Roman devotee,
Sweet virgin Mary I do worship thee'
(*Renascence, A Book of Verse* 1891)

As Isobel Spencer suggests, it is a frank admission of Crane's temporary conversion to the sensualism of Walter Pater and Simeon Solomon. In addition to proclaiming the religion of love it is also a painting about art and the senses. It includes references to all the arts: Painting, Sculpture, Music, Architecture and Poetry as well as the five senses: Sight, Hearing, Touch, Smell and Taste. The eclectic use of Classic, Renaissance, Japanese and Gothic motifs together with, in many of the details, a Pre-Raphaelite fidelity to nature, underlines the freedom felt by Aesthetes to celebrate beauty wherever they found it.

D2 A Herald of Spring 1872
Tempera
622 × 342 mm
Signed with monogram; inscribed:
ROMA APRIL MDCCCLXXII
Birmingham City Museums and Art Gallery

shown with:
(i) *Study for the Figure in 'A Herald of Spring'* 1872
Pencil and charcoal
381 × 253 mm

(ii) *Study for the Background for 'A Herald of Spring'* 1872
Pencil and charcoal
280 × 206 mm
Birmingham City Museums and Art Gallery

According to Crane the twin inspirations for this work were the beauty of the Roman spring, which resulted in a number of landscape studies, and his wife, who was the model for the figure. The drawing of the background shows the Via Sistina with the church of S Trinità dei Monti. The viewpoint in the drawing

D2

appears to have been from a window and this causes some confusion when it is converted to a ground-level view in the finished work. Crane's limitations as a draughtsman are also apparent in the figure study where the relation between the drapery and the underlying figure are unsatisfactory. The problem is not resolved in the finished work, nor is the figure happily related to the background.

D3   At Home – A Portrait   1872
Tempera on paper
710 × 407 mm
Signed with monogram; inscribed:
ROMA/WC MDCCCLXX/II
Leeds City Art Galleries
(plate IV)

At Home is a portrait of Mary Frances Crane painted in Rome in 1872. As with many of Crane's portraits much of the interest lies in the setting. The tiles, a common feature in the Toy Books, are from the artist's imagination as is the hunting tapestry which features Mary dressed as Diana, and behind her a cupid firing an arrow at a crane. The fireplace and the mirror were probably part of the furnishings of the Roman apartment which they rented and the vase, inscribed *Maria*, was of a type which Crane admired.

D4   The Renascence of Venus   1877
Tempera and oil(?) on canvas
1384 × 1841 mm
Signed and dated: *WALTER CRANE*
MDCCCXXVII
The Trustees of the Tate Gallery
(ill p19)

This large and ambitious subject painting was produced for the first Grosvenor Gallery exhibition in 1877. The painting's size and prominent position made it difficult to ignore. Crane collected the reviews and published them in the *Reminiscences* (p174). On the whole they were favourable; they commented in particular on the colouring and the 'feeling for ornamental beauty'. One common criticism was the central nude figure, which Frederic Leighton claimed to be based on a life study of a male model, Alessandro di Marco. The often-repeated story that Crane was forbidden to study from the female figure by his wife might explain some of the uncomfortable aspects of the figure's anatomy, although the simple fact of Crane's lack of formal academic teaching is more convincing. Later on in Crane's career, life drawing was not so much outlawed by a jealous wife as made redundant by a change in his approach to composition and invention.

The question of the medium of this work is one which has troubled critics over the years. Even during Crane's lifetime the condition of the painting had deteriorated and led one obiturist wrongly to suggest that it had been painted in a 'mixed' media of watercolour and gouache. In a letter to Crane, Mrs Russell Barrington, having seen the work in the house of G F Watts (who had bought it from Crane) noted how 'we speculate how far it is tempera and how far oil' (Crane, *Reminiscences* p232). The way in which the paint has sunk into the canvas and the colours changed suggests that Crane was experimenting with a mixed media; speed of execution may have caused further problems.

The subject, indeed the style and execution, was heavily influenced by the work of Botticelli which Crane had first admired in Florence in 1871, in particular the *Birth of Venus* and *Primavera*. Crane's meaning was sufficiently clear for Michael Rossetti to sum up the subject in his review: 'The Rebirth of Beauty; Venus as the symbol of beauty, reborn at the period of art and culture' (Crane, *Reminiscences* p147). The broken temple and the shattered statue are reminders of the glories of the past which, in Crane's optimistic reading, were to be renewed.

D5   Portrait of Lionel and Beatrice Crane   1879
Oil on canvas
480 × 965 mm
Signed with monogram; inscribed and dated: *PINX 1879*
Anthony Crane

D5

shown with:
(i-ii) *Two Studies for 'Portrait of Lionel and Beatrice Crane'* 1879
Pencil and chalk
each 175 × 120 mm oval
Inscribed: *Lionel June 12th; Beatrice June 3rd*
Anthony Crane

Crane used the seated profile format on a number of occasions including the portrait he painted in 1877 of the two daughters of George Routledge, the publisher of the Toy Books. In this portrait of his two eldest children, Crane shows Beatrice reading aloud from a book, with his own *The House That Jack Built* Toy Book on the floor.

D6   Portrait of Beatrice Crane   1880
Oil on canvas
550 × 400 mm
Signed with monogram; dated 1880
Anthony Crane

shown with:
(i) Thomas Crane (1808–1859)
Portrait of Walter Crane as a Child, Aged Three
1848
Oil on canvas
420 × 345 mm oval
Anthony Crane

Crane may have been encouraged to depict members of his family by the set of family portraits, including this one of Crane himself, painted by his father. The forty years which separate the two images underline the changes in attitudes towards children noted by Joany Hichberger. Striking too is the contrast in the furnishings of the two interiors; the latter includes a screen made up from Crane's embossed leather wallpaper *Peacocks and Amorini* (J3) and a sample of the *Swan and Iris* dado wallpaper.

D7   The Angel of Peace (also known as 'A Stranger')   1900
Oil on canvas
1524 × 813 mm
Signed and dated: *Walter Crane 1900*
William Morris Gallery, Walthamstow

In the years around the turn of the century Crane was particularly concerned with agitation for peace and campaigned against the Boer War. It was clear to Crane that war 'was really entered upon in the interests of the gold and diamond mine-owners of the Rand, who were able by their control of the press ... to prejudice the public mind' (Crane, *Reminiscences*

D6

D7

D8   L'Art Et La Vie   1907
Oil on canvas
1524 × 787 mm
Signed with monogram; dated: *MCMVII*
Pre-Raphaelite Inc

p460). Crane's view was in the minority and was not even held by all socialists; disagreement on the issue lead to his resignation from the Fabian group.

The painting shows an angel floating above a globe; she carries an olive branch and recoils in horror from the scene she sees below. She is the *Angel of Peace* but, as the political situation in 1900 indicated, she was also *A Stranger* and hence Crane's alternative title. Two years later Crane drew a cartoon for the *Daily News* in which the angel has alighted and crowns the two bruised and bandaged combatants with an olive branch.

Art is shown holding a mirror to Life in one of Crane's more literal allegories.

GREG SMITH

E Masques and Theatricals

E1

In a career as diverse as Crane's it is not surprising that he sooner or later turned to designing for the stage. He worked on two professional productions, *The Snowman* 1899 and a series of *tableaux vivants* which he designed to accompany Professor Warr's translation of selections from Homer and the *Oresteia* (A39).

Crane was a keen theatre-goer, and was an early champion of Ibsen. In the *Reminiscences* he talks of the 'unflinching way in which Ibsen deals with modern life and tears the mask from the shams and conventionalities of middle-class existence and bourgeois morality'. In the same paragraph Crane goes on to explain

his rather different beliefs. 'The dramatist shatters and destroys, too, without any definite aims of reconstruction …' but people 'will want other sides of life and humanity – the search for a new harmony, a higher sense of beauty' (p336).

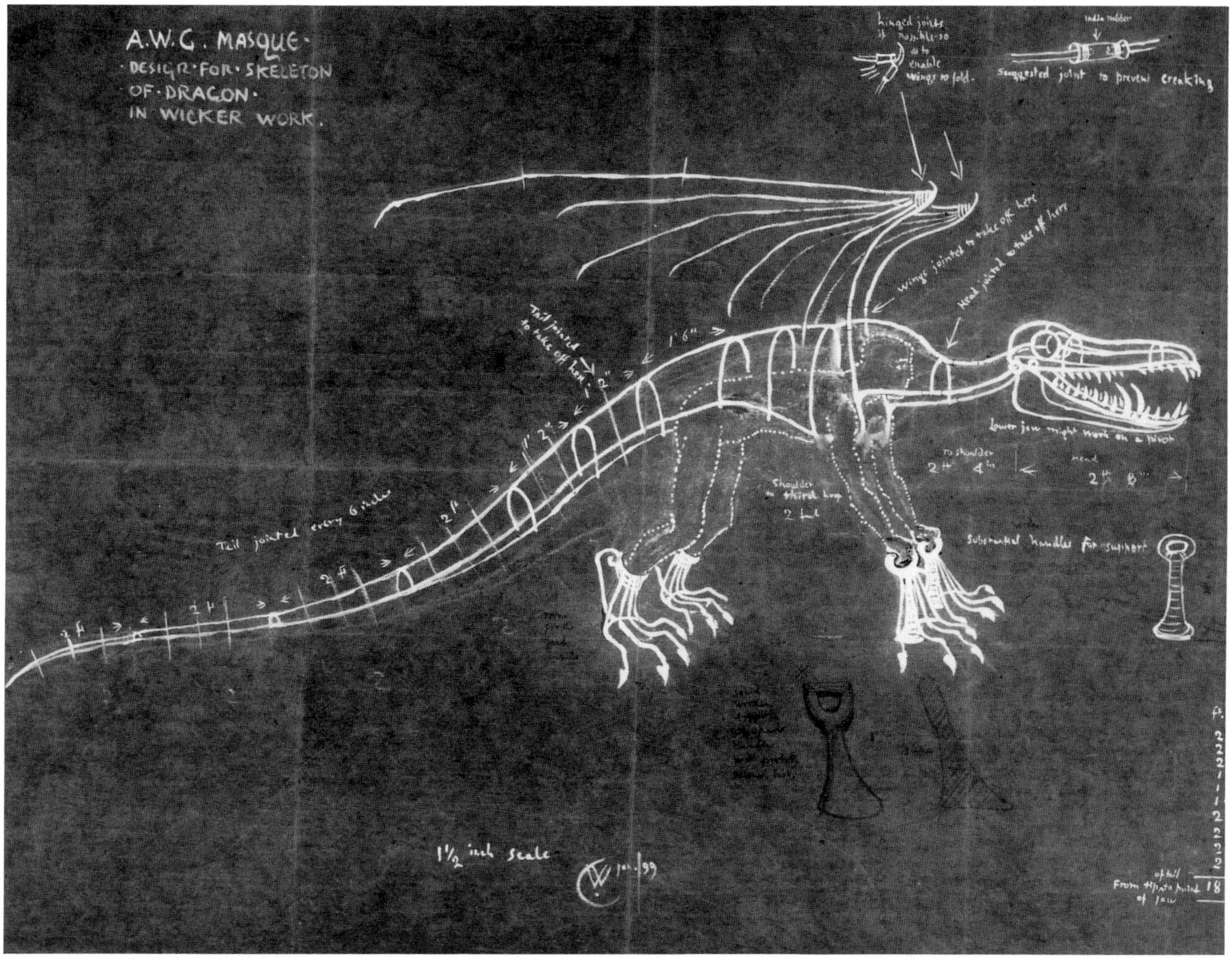

A.W.G. MASQUE.
·DESIGN·FOR·SKELETON·
OF·DRAGON·
IN·WICKER·WORK.

1½ inch scale

E2iv

Crane's interest in the masque first found expression in a book, *The First of May – A Fairy Masque* (A37). It was the perfect vehicle for Crane's ideas as the form itself was based on two of his principal ideals: the unity and fusion of the arts and the superiorty of the allegorical mode of expression. In the prologue to *Beauty's Awakening*, the masque which Crane and his fellow Art Workers' Guild members performed in the Guildhall in 1899, Crane set out his aims: 'DESIGN, then, instead of Illusion: something good (we hope) in Form and Colour and Fancy, & something perhaps worth thought in Allegory and Moral Meaning'.

E1   The Apotheosis of Italian Art
1885–6
Watercolour and gouache
612 × 763 mm
Signed and dated: *Walter Crane 1885–6*
Exh: Grosvenor Gallery, 1886 (16)
Manchester City Art Galleries

This watercolour is a record of a *tableau vivant* which Crane organised as part of the celebrations to mark the reorganisation of the Institute of Painters in Watercolour in 1885. The idea was to represent the different epochs in art in a historical pageant. Crane designed three groups: *Rome*, *Florence* and *Venice* representing the Arts of Italy. The Crane family featured prominently: Mary took the part of Laura, Beatrice an angel, Lionel the young

Giotto, whilst Crane himself was Cimabue. Crane was particularly pleased with his costume and it was illustrated in an article on dress under the heading *Modern and Medieval Simplicity*. The watercolour was commissioned by Henry Irving.

E2   Six Designs for 'Beauty's Awakening: A Masque of Winter and Spring' 1899

(i) *Costume Design: The Spirit of the Age*
Gouache
280 × 229 mm
Signed with monogram; inscribed:
THE SPIRIT OF THE AGE
William Morris Gallery, Walthamstow

(ii) *Study for Miss Johnstone as Nuremberg*
Watercolour and bodycolour
605 × 477 mm
Signed with monogram; dated: Jy 15
1899; inscribed: *Nuremberg*
The Board of Trustees of the Victoria and
Albert Museum, London

(iii) *Study for Baroness de Bertouche as London*
Watercolour and bodycolour
642 × 456 mm
Signed with monogram; dated: July 4 '99;
inscribed: *London*
The Board of Trustees of the Victoria and
Albert Museum, London

(iv) *Design for a Skeleton for Aschemon, a Dragon*
Gouache
560 × 735 mm
Signed with monogram and dated:
Jan '99; inscribed: *A W G MASQUE/
DESIGN FOR SKELETON/OF DRAGON/
IN WICKER WORK*
Royal Borough of Kensington and Chelsea
Library and Arts Service
(ill previous page)

(v) *Study of Trueheart Asleep*
Gouache
560 × 735 mm
Royal Borough of Kensington and Chelsea
Library and Arts Service

(vi) Henry Wilson (1864–1934)
Stage Setting
Gouache
863 × 560 mm
Signed with monogram
The Art Workers' Guild, London

The idea for the masque was Crane's and
was suggested 'by the story of the
Sleeping Beauty, which was made an
allegory of the revival of the arts and the
new Ideal of Life in our time' (Crane,
Reminiscences p452). The story tells how the
Knight Trueheart revives the Spirit of
Beauty, Fayremonde, who has been put to
sleep by Malebodia and, with the help of
Hope and Fortitude, how he defeats the
dragon Aschemon. With Fayremonde
properly enthroned with Trueheart at her
side and the Seven Lamps relit the reign
of beauty can begin. London, hitherto
shown tattered and dejected, is restored
to her true beauty and takes her place
with the nine fair cities of the past.

The masque was appropriately enough
performed in the Guildhall in the City of
London in front of the 'Lord Mayor of
London, Sheriffs, Aldermen, & Common
Council'. What the assembled dignatories
made of the explicit attack on materialism
which was at the heart of the masque's
message is not clear:
'One yet remains, in mean attire, distrest
Though holding riches more than all the
    rest –
E'en London, blackened with the smoke
    of toil
And luxury, and tangled in the moil
Of penury and care, mid wealth untold,
With rich historic garment torn and old'
The message was, however, sweetened as
is the nature of the masque. The work
involved the efforts of a formidable team
of designers. In addition to Crane, who
played a leading role as chairman (as a
player he took the part of Albrecht
Dürer), the other major contributors
were C R Ashbee, Selwyn Image,
Harrison Townsend, C W Whall and
Henry Wilson. The text and many
illustrations were printed in *The Studio
Summer Number* 1899.

GREG SMITH

F   The Promotion of Art and Design: Theory and Practice

Although Crane was always interested in art and design theory it was not until the mid-1880s that his espousal of the socialist cause and his work for the Arts and Crafts Exhibition Society led him to take on a greater burden of lecture and teaching commitments. This took the form of papers of a theoretical nature such as 'Art and Social Democracy' and 'Art and Commercialism' (reprinted in *The Claims of Decorative Art*) and lectures on specific areas of craft and design which, although they often had an historical component, were essentially practical.

As many have testified, Crane's greatest gift as a teacher lay in the use he made of visual aids. He carefully prepared large-scale drawings to illustrate points as well as executing rapid 'on the spot' drawings on the blackboard. Much of the point of the exercise came after the lecture, when students had the chance to look more closely at the images. Crane did not use 'lantern slides' until his lectures of 1889 on the decorative illustration of books, and used photographs only to illustrate historical points. Many of the diagrams were reworked for reproduction in *The Bases of Design* 1895 and *Line and Form* 1900. The text of those influential books was based on the two sets of lectures which he gave in the capacity of Director of Design at the School of Art in Manchester.

Before taking up the post in 1893 Crane published a series of *Recommendations and Suggestions for Adoption either as distinct from, or in addition to the Present System … with reference to the Study and Practice of Design*. These were followed to varying degrees but, given the necessity for all examined work to be submitted to the National Art Training School at South Kensington, they were a help only to some of the more talented and open-minded students and remained an optional extra.

Walter Crane '*What is Art?*' from '*The Quarto*' 1898

Some of Crane's more adventurous ideas included the encouragement of bi-manual skills, the provision of an aviary to improve colour study, the move away from static poses in the life class and the introduction of elements of comparative anatomy. The School's collection of teaching materials and exhibits, especially of the Arts and Crafts movement, was greatly expanded under Crane and was opened as a museum in 1898.

F1 Seven Lecture Diagrams adapted for 'The Bases of Design'   c1893–8
Titles inscribed on drawings in Crane's hand

(i) *'Corbel 14th Cent. Dennington Church. Suffolk.' Lecture III. Of the Influence of Material and Method*
Watercolour and gouache
740 × 560 mm

(ii) *'Wood Carving. Miserere, St David's Cathedral.' Lecture III. Of the Influence of Material and Method*
Watercolour and gouache
740 × 560 mm

(iii) *'Porch of Cathedral of S. Jacopo Pistoia.' Lecture V. Of the Climatic Influence in Design*
Watercolour and gouache
760 × 555 mm
Signed with monogram

(iv) *'Arabian XIVth Century Carved and Inlaid Pulpit, Cairo (South Kensington Museum). Drawn by W. Cleobury.' Lecture VI. Of the Racial Influence in Design*
Watercolour
790 × 540 mm

(v) *'Polynesian Ornament from Hervey Island Paddle.' Lecture VII. Of the Symbolic Influence, or Emblematic Element in Design*
Ink and wash
760 × 560 mm

(vi) *'Interior of the Atelier of Etienne Delaune. Paris. 1576.' Lecture X. Of the Collective Influence*
Ink and wash
557 × 710 mm

(vii) *'Interior of a Printing Office in the XIVth Century. From Jost Amman.' Lecture X. Of the Collective Influence*
Ink and wash

F1 iv

733 × 600 mm
Royal Borough of Kensington and Chelsea Library and Arts Service

The first set of lectures took as its main theme the unity of the arts, and the cover of the book stressed this by showing the organisation of the ten bases in the diagrammatic form of a tree. Crane used historical examples not as a compendium of forms to be memorised, but as a source of sound principles to be first learnt, and then applied in practice. Crane's Rationalist approach to the origin of decorative features is evident in the chapters on the climatic and racial influences on design where the use of polychromy in Italian architecture is explained by the flattening effect of the

INTERIOR·OF·THE·ATELIER·OF·ETIENNE·DELAULNE

F1 vi

bright sun and where he argues that the Muslim faith 'turned the ingenuity and invention … in a purely ornamental direction' (Crane, *Bases* p206).

Crane's belief in the workshop as the ideal expression of the 'necessity of intelligent and artistic co-operation' (Crane, *Bases* p352), of the continuity and develop-ment of skills and the best place to learn an art or craft skill is illustrated in F1 vi-vii.

F2   Five Lecture Diagrams adapted for 'Line and Form'   c1893–1900
Titles inscribed on drawings in Crane's hand

(i) *'Silhouette of Beech Leaves and Line Rendering of the Same Thing.' Chapter I*
Ink and wash
760 × 555 mm

(ii) *'Olive Branch from Nature.' Chapter II.*
Converted from a Study of an Olive Branch
Watercolour
548 × 380 mm
Signed with monogram; inscribed and dated: *VIA APPIA ROMA OCT XX*
MDCCCLXXI

(iii) *'Olive Branch Simplified in Decorative Treatment.' Chapter II*
Ink and wash
760 × 555 mm
Signed with monogram

(iv) *'Constructive Line Re-Echoed in Architectural Ornament. Corbel, Bishop Vaughan's Chapel, St. David's 1509.' Chapter V*
Ink and wash
560 × 730 mm
Signed with monogram

(v) *'Controlling Line in Design of Subsidiary Architectural Decoration. c1460–1480 Wood Carving, Miserere Seat, Choir Stalls, St David's Cathedral.' Chapter V*
Ink and wash and chalk
560 × 730 mm
Signed with monogram

(i,iii,iv,v) Royal Borough of Kensington and Chelsea Library and Arts Service
(ii) Anthony Crane

The second set of lectures was more practical and complemented the exercises set down in the *Recommendations and Suggestions*. Emphasis was placed on the range and possiblities of line, with a detailed analysis of the nature of pattern

and decoration. F2ii was converted from a life study made in Italy and was contrasted with the same form treated decoratively. The drawings demonstrate the distinction between the 'graphic purpose', the accidental form taken from nature and the 'ornamental purpose', the typical form suitable for decoration (see also ill p40).

The origin of decorative forms in architecture was one of the major themes of Crane's theories on design. Examples of decoration used in Gothic architecture were used to illustrate 'complexity within unity', each element being determined by its relation to the whole.

The Arts and Crafts Exhibition Society

Crane played a leading role in the activities of both 'The Fifteen', founded in 1881 at the instigation of Lewis F Day, and the Art Workers' Guild, formed in 1884. Both organisations proved a valuable meeting forum for like-minded designers but they did not act, as Crane wished, as a public focus for reform. Crane was one of those designers and artists who lobbied for a National Exhibition for the Arts and which would include the applied arts. When, however, it was decided to try and work with the Royal Academy Crane, who regarded it as unreformable, resigned and with a group which included W A S Benson, L F Day and T J Cobden-Sanderson founded The Arts and Crafts Exhibition Society.

The first exhibition was held in the autumn of 1888, then annually until 1890 when it became triennial. It departed from the trade exhibitions, the only place applied art had been shown before, in two notable respects: in the emphasis placed on the designer and the executant rather than the manufacturer, and in the avowedly didactic nature of the display, which included exhibits such as Edmund Evans' stage proofs which illustrated working methods, and the lectures, demonstrations and catalogue essays which accompanied the exhibition.

F3   Design for the Letterhead for The Arts and Crafts Exhibition Society
Pen and ink
120 × 410 mm
Signed with monogram
The Board of Trustees of the Victoria and Albert Museum, London

F4   Design for the Entrance to the Arts and Crafts Exhibition Society
Watercolour and gouache on tracing paper
375 × 380 mm (irregular)
Royal Borough of Kensington and Chelsea Library and Arts Service

The design for an entrance to the exhibition was not carried out. The frieze and panel designs, like the letterhead, include allegorical representations of Handicraft and Design.

GREG SMITH

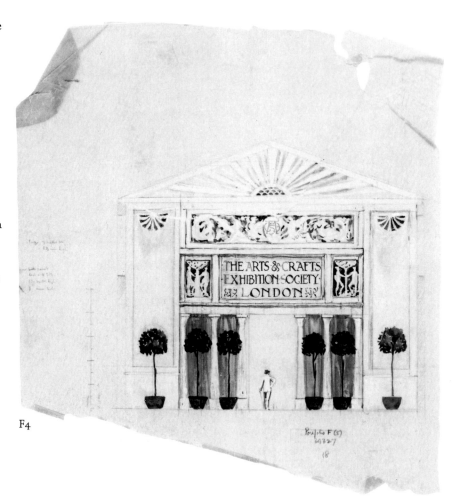

F4

G   Interior Decoration

Early schemes

**G1   Design for a Door Surround,
South Kensington Museum**   1870s
Watercolour and pencil
580 × 392 mm
Royal Borough of Kensington and Chelsea
Library and Arts Service

**G2   Design for a Room Decoration
for 11 Palace Gardens**   mid-1870s
Watercolour and pencil on tracing paper
255 × 373 mm
Inscribed: *J de Murrieta Eq, 11 Palace Gardens,
Kensington*
Royal Borough of Kensington and Chelsea
Library and Arts Service

Both of these early schemes went no
further than this stage, though Crane did
execute a frieze decoration of birds and
animals for Palace Gardens.

**G3   Design for a Painted Ceiling at
Wortley Hall, Yorkshire: 'Night and
Day'**   c1876
Watercolour, gouache, gold paint on
brown paper
556 × 342 mm
Whitworth Art Gallery, University of
Manchester
(ill p51)

Sir Edward Poynter, who had finished
two large paintings for the Billiard Room
at Wortley Hall, recommended Crane to
Lord Wharncliffe in 1876 to complete the
decorations. Crane visited Wortley in
November 1876 and 'on returning home,
I made a coloured sketch for the ceiling
and frieze … with Night and Day and the
Hours' (Crane, *Reminiscences* p173). Crane's
memory was faulty; the design shows the
months divided by the signs of the
zodiac. The scheme was not realised.

Walter Crane *Page from 'Aladdin'* (A20)

**Interior decoration and
the Toy Books**

The majority of the Toy Books were set
in the past and in different countries and
required Crane's wide knowledge of the
collections at South Kensington to devise
the complex and imaginative interior
settings. In the *Reminiscences* Crane admitted

that 'I had my fun out of them, as in
designing I was in the habit of putting in
all sorts of subsidiary detail … and often
made them the vehicle for my ideas in
furniture and decoration' (p156). Often
they were put together with a degree of
historical and geographical latitude. The
conflation of the very different cultures of

Walter Crane *Page from 'Little Queen Anne'* (A28)

Crane's views on interior decoration and his thoughts on the work of his contemporaries in the Arts and Crafts movement. The letter inviting Crane to design rooms to show 'English style ... of the best kind' arrived in December 1892. The company intended to create '30–40 furnished rooms ... [of] different prices and styles, from middle to highest class goods' and invited Crane to Germany. Instead Crane chose three from a list of twelve suggestions of rooms and styles: a Billiard Room and Library, a Bedroom in the 'English Empire' style and a Dressing Room.

Crane sent off his annotated designs with addresses of suppliers and samples of materials in February. His bill for £300 was returned however in a letter of 27 March 1893, with the comment that the designs 'are of no value for German taste'. In the ensuing correspondence, Crane claimed that he normally charged £5 5s a day for examination work and 'in my ordinary professional work my fee is easily doubled'. In the end the drawings were returned and the fee halved.

G4   Four Drawings for a Billiard Room and Library for Gerson & Co
1892–3
Each drawing inscribed with title and specifications in Crane's hand

(i) *FIRE PLACE SIDE: BILLIARD ROOM & LIBRARY: DESIGNED BY WALTER CRANE*
Scale 8¾ cent to 1 metre or 1 inch to 1 foot
– English Measure
Frieze in relief tinted plaster
Wall in stamped and gilded wall paper – pattern 'Corona Vitae' (Jeffrey & Co.)
Repoussé brass dishes – (Guild & School of Handicraft)
Book shelves in stained oak
Carved heraldic hounds with copper banners
Lustre tiles (De-Morgan & Co)
Lustre pottery (Maw & Co)
Cast iron grate back and wrought iron and brass fire dogs (W. A. S. Benson & Co.)
Pen and brown ink over pencil with white wash
455 × 605 mm

the Near and Far East and Japan and China in *Aladdin* 1875 (A20, plate IX, ill p119) and *Ali Baba* 1873 are typical of the 19th century. Likewise a French château in *Beauty and the Beast* 1874 (A19) and an Italian Renaissance palazzo in *Cinderella* 1873 are not always matched correctly to costume. This however is not the point; Crane clearly enjoyed allowing his imagination to run freely and they give the right sense of location and atmosphere without being pedantic. As for period, the stories themselves were not historical and Crane's details convey a sense of the past without being specific.

At least two of Crane's books refer to the fashionable 'Queen Anne' style of the 1870s. In *The Three Bears* 1873, Crane illustrates a perfect Queen Anne interior

with homely cottage kitchen and all the most fashionable furniture. The traditional English garden is also well stocked with sunflowers. These also appear in *Little Queen Anne* 1886 (A28), which shows a young girl dressed in Kate Greenaway style in front of her Queen Anne dolls' house.

Rooms for a showroom for Gerson & Co

The rediscovery in the collection of Kensington Public Library of the drawings, correspondence and specifications of a group of showrooms designed by Crane for the German firm of Gerson & Co of Berlin provide an important source of information on

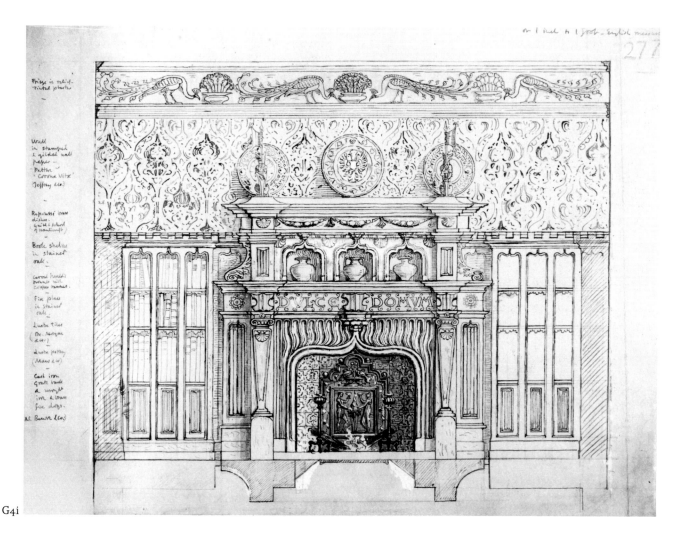

G4i

(ii) *2 WINDOW SIDE: BILLIARD ROOM & LIBRARY: DESIGNED BY WALTER CRANE*
Scale 8¾ centimetres to 1 metre or 1 inch to 1 foot English Measure
Window in leaded quarries of antique glass with stained glass panels above
2 annotated plans on the drawing
Pen and brown ink over pencil with white wash
455 × 605 mm
(ill next page)

(iii) *4. BILLIARD ROOM & LIBRARY. DESIGNED BY WALTER CRANE. SETTLE SIDE*
Scale 8¾ cents to 1 metre or 1 inch to 1 foot English measure
Settle in stained oak with carved canopy and painted panel.
Tapestry hangings and book shelves.

Carved oak chairs with stamped velvet cushions.
Brass sconces.
Pen and brown ink over pencil
455 × 605 mm

(iv) *5 DOOR SIDE: BILLIARD ROOM & LIBRARY: DESIGNED BY WALTER CRANE.*
Scale 8¾ centimetres to 1 metre – or inch to 1 foot. English measure
Pen and brown ink over pencil
455 × 605 mm
Royal Borough of Kensington and Chelsea Library and Arts Service

G5   Four Drawings for a Bedroom for Gerson & Co   1892–3
Each drawing inscribed with the title and specifications in Crane's hand

(i) *BEDROOM* (English Empire) 1
Wall paper 'Rose' (Jeffrey & Co. London)

Corner cupboard if space enough
Recessed window if room
PLAN OF CORNER CUPBOARD
PLAN OF WASHBAND TOP
PLAN OF HANGING WARDROBE
WINDOW RECESS
Pen and black ink over pencil and white wash
452 × 665 mm
(ill p123)

(ii) *BEDROOM* (English Empire) 2
Scale – 1 metre
Annotated plan
Pen and black ink over pencil
453 × 658 mm

(iii) *BEDROOM* (English Empire) 3
Wallpaper 'Rose' (Jeffrey & Co. London)
'Dove' ceiling paper
Scale: 1 metre

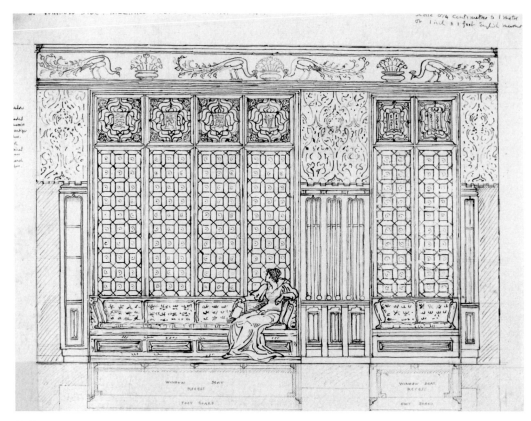

G4ii

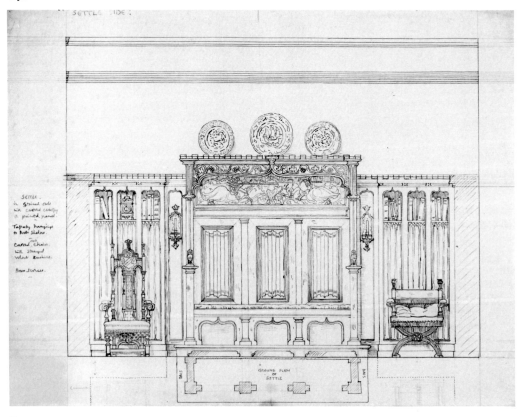

G4iii

G5i

PLAN OF CUPBOARD ½ PLAN OF SOFA
Pen and black ink over pencil and black
and white wash
453 × 661 mm

(iv) *BEDROOM* (English Empire) 4
Scale 1 metre
Annotated plan
Pen and black ink over pencil
451 × 661 mm

shown with:
(v) Two Colour Keys with Swatches of
Material
Royal Borough of Kensington and Chelsea
Library and Arts Service

The Bedroom designs are in the more
attenuated, 'feminine' style of 'English
Empire' in contrast to the 'male' Jacobean
style of the Billiard Room and Library.
The specifications and samples also
include from Morris & Co: 'Muslin
Curtains – No 151', a carpet 'Wilton –
C or E 6028' and a textile, *Marigold*. The
dressing-room designs, not shown,
include other Morris textiles 'No 3/1771'
'carpet 1/5314' as well as Crane's *Peacock
Garden* (J13) wallpaper and a screen made
from a leather peacock pattern.

JOANNA BANHAM
GREG SMITH

H Textiles

H2

Crane referred to textiles as 'the most intimate of the arts of design' (Crane, *Bases* p102) because of their close association with daily life. Yet, although he produced designs at some stage for almost every branch of textile art, he never developed his ideas in these media to the full. His introduction to textiles probably came from his wife Mary who, in common with most women of her class, was a skilled amateur embroideress. During the 1870s Crane became involved

with the Royal School of Art Needlework. Set up in 1872 and run by a committee of philanthropically-minded aristocratic ladies, the school's aims were to supply suitable employment for needy gentle-women and to improve standards of orna-mental needlework. Crane produced a number of designs for them, including the large and prestigious embroideries which hung at the entrance to the school's stand at the Philadelphia Centennial Exposition of 1876.

Crane identified two sorts of pattern in textiles: that which is incorporated (as in weaving), and that which is applied to the surface (as in printing). Of the two it was the latter, he felt, which allowed the designer greater freedom. 'There is no doubt that with patterns printed more range may be allowed than with patterns to be woven' (Crane, *Line* p248). Crane used this freedom to produce highly distinctive printed textile designs. Arguably though, they are too much of a

H3

good thing when put into repeat over a long length, and certainly they work less well when draped in folds than smaller-scale floral or more abstract patterns.

Weaving placed more technical limitations on the designer, 'since the design must be capable of being rendered upon the severe conditions of the point paper, by which it is only possible to produce curves by small successive angles' and a certain 'squareness of mass becomes a desirable and characteristic

feature' (Crane, *Line* p62). Some of Crane's most successful textile designs, critically and commercially, however, were for weaving. Morris & Co reproduced a design of Crane's, *The Goose Girl*, in traditional arras tapestry in 1881 but he received no further work in this line. This is a pity, since Crane's figurative style and his observance of the need in tapestry to reduce the number of planes in a picture and remove chiaroscuro effects, lent themselves well to this most pictorial of the textile arts.

H1   The British Empire   1887
Machine-printed cotton
Manufactured by Edmund Potter & Co
754 × 533 mm
The Board of Trustees of the Victoria and Albert Museum, London

H2   Fanfare of Fashions   1887
Machine-printed cotton
Manufactured by Edmund Potter & Co
515 × 730 mm
Whitworth Art Gallery, University of Manchester

H4

Both these cottons (H1 and H2) were produced to celebrate Victoria's Jubilee. The *Fanfare of Fashions* was made into a parasol for the Queen. *The British Empire* Crane described as 'a kind of apotheosis of the British Empire expressed in a figurative way' (Crane, *Art Journal* p 15).

H3   The Senses   c1891
Tablecloth and four napkins; linen damask
Manufactured by John Wilson & Sons
Tablecloth 1830 × 1900 mm; Napkins 660 × 740 mm each
Embroidered monogram: *CW* (*WC?*)
Exh: A & C, 1893 with watercolour design
Whitworth Art Gallery, University of Manchester
(ill previous page)

The Senses tablecloth was the most widely illustrated exhibit of the 1893 Arts and Crafts Exhibition, and the most popular of the damask designs commissioned by John Wilson & Sons from contemporary artists. Figures representing the Five Senses occupy the centre of the field, surrounded by a border of animals of the chase. Two subsidiary borders originally bore an inscription. According to Crane (Crane, *Art Journal* p 15), it was objected that the words were reversed because of the necessity of repeating them, and, as in this case, a formalised repeating leaf pattern was substituted. The design is repeated on the napkins, but without the animal border.

H4 (i-ii)   **Flora's Retinue**   c1891
Two sets of six dessert doilys
Coloured silk and linen damask; with box
Manufactured by John Wilson & Sons
Each 178 × 178 mm
Inscribed: *Rose, Lily, Pink, Daisy, Bluebell, Poppy*
Exh: A & C, 1893 (160); Chicago, 1893
(i) Whitworth Art Gallery, University of Manchester
(ii) Anthony Crane

shown with:
(iii) *Design for 'Lily'*
Pencil and gouache
178 × 178 mm
Anthony Crane

These doilys, produced in cream or coloured damask, are closely related to the group of flower books which began with *Flora's Feast* 1889 (A34) and to the later set of tiles *Flora's Retinue* (K9). A letter in the Houghton Library dated August 1891 gives Crane's design fee: £36.

H5   The Four Seasons   1893
Machine-printed Japon silk
Manufactured by Thomas Wardle & Co for Liberty's
785 × 635 mm
Exh: A & C, 1893 (221)
Whitworth Art Gallery, University of Manchester

Crane's study of historic textiles in the South Kensington Museum bore fruit in a number of his textile designs. Here *Opus Anglicanum* embroideries or, more likely, Persian silks have suggested the prominent roundels enclosing the figures. Crane uses a number of silks in an article 'Needlework as a Mode of Artistic Expression' to illustrate the principle of 'controlling shape and borders' (*The Magazine of Art* 1898 pp 147 and 198).

H6   Daffodil and Bluebell   1896
Machine-woven Brussels carpet sample; wool and jute
Manufactured by Templeton and Co
730 × 1117 mm
Inscribed: *Daffodil and Bluebell. Designed by Walter Crane*
Exh: A & C, 1903

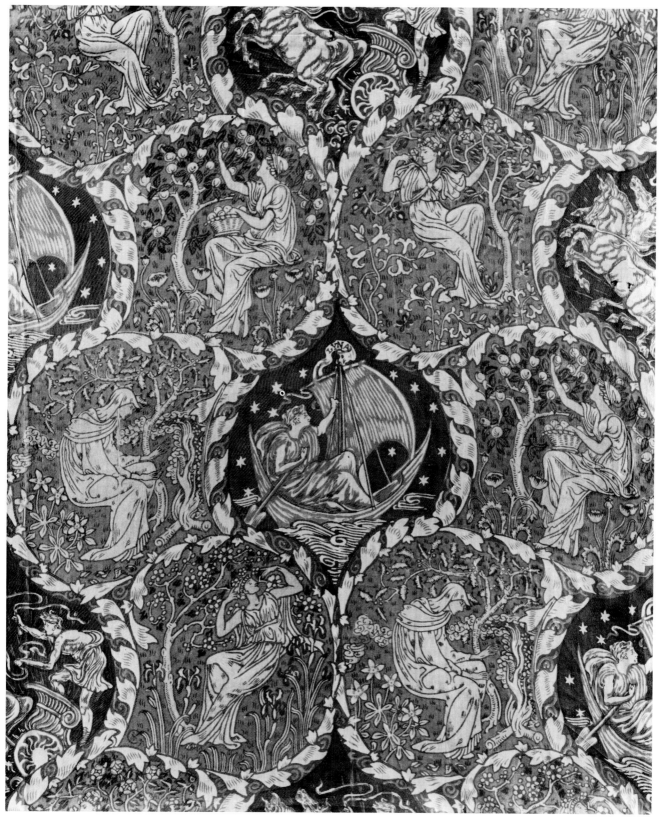

H5

The Board of Trustees of the Victoria and Albert Museum, London

shown with:

(i) *Design for 'Daffodil and Bluebell'* c1895
Watercolour on squared paper
660 × 682 mm
The Board of Trustees of the Victoria and Albert Museum, London

A number of Crane's designs for carpets for the Glasgow company Templeton & Co were shown at the Glasgow exhibition in 1901. They are all resolutely flat in conception and avoid animate forms, unlike the textiles and wallpapers of the same period.

H7   Pheasant and Rose or Golden Pheasant   c1902

Block-printed cotton; printed originally by Birch Gibson, later by Stead McAlpine
1905 × 1300 mm
Whitworth Art Gallery, University of Manchester

The watercolour designs for this and H8 are in the Victoria and Albert Museum; both are dated 1902.

H8   The National Arms of England, Scotland and Ireland   c1902

Block-printed worsted
1970 × 1360 mm
Whitworth Art Gallery, University of Manchester
(ill p45)

H9   Design for a Printed Cotton: 'Iris'   1903

Watercolour
901 × 430 mm
Signed with monogram; dated: '03
The Board of Trustees of the Victoria and Albert Museum, London

H10   England and France   1908

Wool and cotton woven hanging
Woven by A H Lee & Sons for Warner & Sons
2340 × 1430 mm
Exh: Franco-British Exhibition, 1908
Whitworth Art Gallery, University of Manchester
(plate II)

shown with:

(i) *Initial Sketch for 'England and France'*
Pencil and watercolour
Royal Borough of Kensington and Chelsea Library and Arts Service

Crane believed that heraldry had 'a certain decorative value to the designer, as illustrating the principle of counterchange of colours' (Crane, *Bases* p241–2), and that this was particularly relevant in textile design where one wanted to play 'one tint or colour upon another' without creating any sense of depth. Admiring the bold patterning of medieval heraldry Crane sought to revive a tradition which he felt had become fossilised.

H11   'Days of the Week'   c1872–3

Ebonised cabinet with six needlework panels
Designed by Crane; worked by Mary Frances Crane
1500 × 980 × 516 mm
Anthony Crane

The panels which decorate this cabinet were worked in Italy from Crane's designs. Mary Frances was a talented needlewoman and she exhibited her work regularly at the Arts and Crafts Exhibitions.

H12   Scene from 'Aladdin'

Coloured silk embroidery on linen
Designed by Crane; embroidered by G Parkyns (?)
760 × 660 mm
Inscribed: *WALTER CRANE G PARKYNS*
The Board of Trustees of the Victoria and Albert Museum, London

This panel is based on a page for the Toy Book *Aladdin* (A20, plate IX, ill p119).

H13 (i-vii)   Seven Designs for Children's and Women's Clothes

Pencil, pen and some watercolour
Anthony Crane

Crane designed clothes for his family and himself and not surprisingly had strong views on the subject of modern dress,

inclining toward artistic dress based on classical art. His own children were clothed according to the principles of 'utility, simplicity, picturesqueness' and these were also the qualities he valued most in peasant costume.

H14   Peacock Screen   c1875–6

Designed by Crane; executed by students at the Royal School of Art Needlework
Wool on cotton and silk
1511 × 597 mm
Private Collection

H15   London

Book binding; coloured silk embroidery
Designed by Crane; worked by Mary Frances Crane
153 × 115 mm
John Rylands Library, University of Manchester

JENNIFER HARRIS
GREG SMITH

H7

J   Wallpapers

In 1875 Metford Warner asked Crane to produce a design for a hand-printed wallpaper to be displayed on the Jeffrey & Co stand at the Philadelphia Centennial Exposition the following year. The result was a tripartite decoration comprising the *Lily and Dove* dado, *La Margarete* filling (J1), and the *Alcestis* frieze (ill p131). The design won much critical acclaim and a special award for Jeffrey & Co.

The firm had previously exhibited at international exhibitions in London and Paris and, clearly, Warner had realised the value of these promotional events. The success of Jeffrey & Co's display at Philadelphia led to the production of a number of special designs by Crane which contributed largely to the firm's receipt of awards at numerous exhibitions. By the early 1880s his designs had been exhibited widely both as traditional hand-prints and flocked papers, as embossed papers which imitated stamped leather, and as luxurious leather decorations which were gilded, lacquered and hand-painted. Crane's wallpapers were regularly reviewed in both the trade and the popular press and, as he also designed several advertisements for the firm (ill p130), Jeffrey & Co was seen to be at the forefront of 'artistic' production.

Records of the fees paid to Crane for his designs have not survived, and although we know that he received a royalty on orders the evidence suggests that he may have been unique in this respect. It is unlikely that, in terms of sales, Jeffrey & Co found the production of Crane's wallpaper designs as profitable as those produced by the other well-known designers who worked for the firm. However, it was the success of Crane's decoration at Philadelphia which made

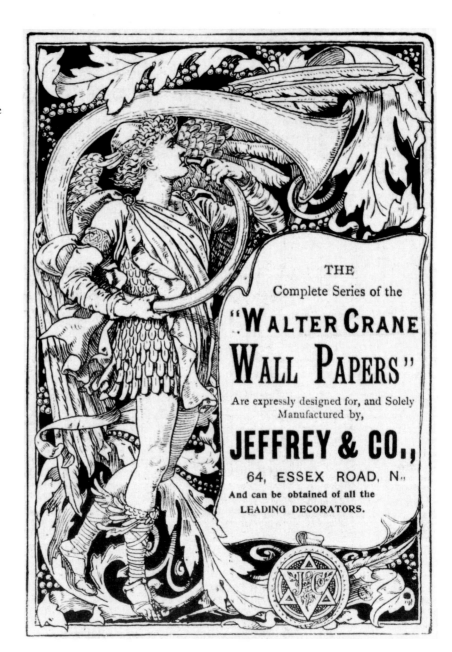

Walter Crane *Advertisement for Jeffrey & Co wallpapers from 'The Art Journal Easter Art Annual'* 1898

Walter Crane 'Alcestis', 'La Margarete', and 'Lily and Dove' decoration
1876, block-printed wallpapers

Warner realise that in future 'there would be no need to go running to Paris for designs' (Metford Warner, *Notes for Art Workers' Guild* 1896 p72).

The success of Jeffrey & Co was due in no small measure to the entrepreneurial flair and sound commercial sense of Metford Warner. However, there is no doubt that it was Crane's work, more than that of any other designer employed by the firm, which led to the establishment of both the artist and his employer as major influences in the British wallpaper industry.

J1 La Margarete 1876
Colour print from woodblocks
864 × 533 mm
The Board of Trustees of the Victoria and Albert Museum, London
(ill previous page)

shown with:
(i) *Wallpaper Log Book c1861−85*
Showing samples of the three designs exhibited.
A Sanderson & Sons Ltd

(ii) *Diploma Awarded to Jeffrey & Co, Philadelphia 1876*
Whitworth Art Gallery, University of Manchester

Inspired by a poem by Chaucer, this design was clearly influenced by Morris' *Daisy*, 1864. Crane remarked that he did not 'expect quotations from Shelley or Chaucer' on wallpapers or carpets, 'albeit I was once guilty of inscribing the refrain from "The flower and the leaf" all over a wall-paper (don't shudder)' (Crane, *Moot Points* p78). *La Margarete*, complete with poem, was exhibited as part of a tripartite decoration at Philadelphia, 1876, where it won an award.

J2 Design for 'Peacocks and Amorini' 1878
Watercolour
1067 × 531 mm
The Board of Trustees of the Victoria and Albert Museum, London

This design shows the scheme both for flat printing and embossed leather paper.

J2

J5

The production of *Peacocks and Amorini* as an imitation leather decoration was an experiment carried out with a view to display at the Paris Exhibition, 1878, where it was shown with a complementary frieze and dado, and won a gold medal. The design was also produced as a stamped leather decoration (J3).

J3 Peacocks and Amorini 1878
Embossed leather lacquered in gold
1585 × 533 mm
Leeds City Art Galleries

Real leather decorations such as this one were considerably more expensive than the embossed leather papers although the difference between them was said to be 'very difficult to detect'.

J4 Billow 1879
Colour print from woodblocks
533 × 457 mm
The Board of Trustees of the Victoria and Albert Museum, London

Billow was issued with the *Mermaid* frieze and a dado 'representing the pebbly sea-bottom, with starfish, shells, etc'. The *Scallop Shell* ceiling paper was designed to complete the decorative scheme.

J5 Sleeping Beauty 1879
Colour machine print
850 × 535 mm
The Board of Trustees of the Victoria and Albert Museum, London

The British Architect (23 May 1884 p225) said: 'It is not necessary to point out to our readers how gracefully and simply Mr Crane tells the tales of fairy kind and nursery rhyme. With the aid of a little intelligent and sympathetic talk nursery walls, covered with these designs, might be made to *live* in the lives of children.' (ill previous page)

J6 Awakening Day 1880
Colour print from woodblocks
864 × 508 mm
Whitworth Art Gallery, University of Manchester

J6

Designed as a 'staircase paper' with a
pattern of hounds, hunting-horns, cocks
and doves, etc, to 'carry out the idea of
awakening day' (Studio, 1894–5 p77).

J7   The House That Jack Built   1886
Colour machine print
3600 × 535 mm
John Dennis
(ill p61)

Crane's fifth machine-printed nursery
paper.

J8   Woodnotes   1886
Colour print from woodblocks
864 × 508 mm
Whitworth Art Gallery, University of
Manchester
(ill p63)

shown with:
(i) *Sheet of Studies for 'Woodnotes'*
Pencil and watercolour
Royal Borough of Kensington and Chelsea
Library and Arts Service

The *Woodnotes* filling was inspired by a
passage in *As You Like It*:
'Under the greenwood tree
Who loves to lie with me,
And turn his merry note
Unto the sweet bird's throat,'
Its large and ambitious pattern, which
required eighteen blocks, marked a new
phase in Crane's style and from 1886
animals and figures assumed a more
important role in his wallpaper designs.

J9   Deer and Rabbits   1887
Colour print from woodblocks
527 × 508 mm
Whitworth Art Gallery, University of
Manchester
(ill p42)

shown with:
(i) *Tracing for 'Deer and Rabbits'*
Pencil and ink on tracing paper
Royal Borough of Kensington and Chelsea
Library and Arts Service

A wallpaper frieze for use with the
Woodnotes filling.

J13

J10   The Golden Age   1887
Colour print from woodblocks
864 × 508 mm
Whitworth Art Gallery, University of
Manchester

In 1886 Crane explained his intention in
this design as being 'to suggest all manner
of pleasant things' (Jeffrey & Co Log
Books Vol I p63).

J11   The Golden Age   1887
Embossed leather paper
1370 × 525 mm
Manchester City Art Galleries
(plate III)

Jeffrey & Co regarded the embossed
leather version of The Golden Age as the
most important new imitation leather
decoration of 1887.

This example was originally hung in the
library at Wythenshawe Hall, and can
now be seen re-hung at Fletcher Moss
Museum, Manchester.

J12   The Victorian Series   1889
Wallpaper catalogue
342 × 238 mm
Manchester Polytechnic Library

The Victorian Series was a collection of
designs of slightly larger scale than
ordinary patterns and included designs
by Crane, Day, Sedding, and others.
The design of the catalogue itself was
described as 'quite a departure from any
English book' hitherto issued (British
Architect 8 February 1889). The cover was
designed by Crane.

J13   Peacock Garden   1889
Colour print from woodblocks
1235 × 545 mm
Whitworth Art Gallery, University of
Manchester
(ill on previous page)

shown with:
(i) Tracing for 'Peacock Garden'
Pencil and ink on tracing paper
Anthony Crane

(ii-vi) Five Studies for a Peacock Filling and Frieze
Pencil and watercolour

Royal Borough of Kensington and Chelsea
Library and Arts Service

Peacock Garden was first exhibited in 1889
printed in several shades of flock, the
colours of which had been blended in 'a
quite unique way' (The Building News 20
December 1889). It was also shown as a
gilded and lacquered decoration.

J14   White Peacock   1889
Colour print from woodblocks
533 × 508 mm
Whitworth Art Gallery, University of
Manchester

A wallpaper frieze for use with the Peacock
Garden filling. The decoration was awarded
a gold medal at the Paris Exhibition 1889.

J15   Corona Vitae   1890
Colour print from woodblocks
Frieze: 610 × 508 mm
Filling: 1235 × 552 mm
Whitworth Art Gallery, University of
Manchester
(ill p43)

Inspired by Sicilian silk hangings, the
Corona Vitae decoration was one of Crane's
most elaborate essays in wallpaper design.
The decoration was also produced as an
embossed leather.

J16   Four Winds   1890
Colour print from woodblocks
940 × 533 mm
Whitworth Art Gallery, University of
Manchester
(ill p138)
A ceiling paper for use with the Corona
Vitae decoration. The drawing of it
required, Crane recalled, 'particular pains
and care' (Studio, 1894-5 p78).

J17   Pomegranate and Teazle   1894
Colour print from woodblocks
711 × 520 mm
Whitworth Art Gallery, University of
Manchester

shown with:
(i) Sketch for a Pomegranate Pattern
Pencil and watercolour
Royal Borough of Kensington and Chelsea
Library and Arts Service

One of two designs produced after Crane
had been asked to reduce the number of
colours; Pomegranate and Teazle required only
four blocks and was one of the cheapest
of his wallpapers at 6½d per yard.

J18   Lily and Rose   1894
Colour print from woodblocks
565 × 530 mm (fragment)
The National Trust

Designed in 1894 after Crane had been
asked to reduce the number of colours in
his designs, Lily and Rose required four
blocks for the design plus one for the
optional backprint.

J19   Lily and Rose   1987
Colour screen print
1210 × 555 mm
Whitworth Art Gallery, University of
Manchester
(ill p66)

shown with:
(i) Photograph of the design being
printed at the Sanderson works at Brook
Mill, Lower Darwen (courtesy
A Sanderson & Sons Ltd)

(ii) Photograph of the reprinted Lily and
Rose, in situ in the Huntroyde Room,
Gawthorpe Hall (courtesy Country Life)

The blocks for Lily and Rose have not
survived and in 1987 the design was
transferred to screens and reprinted by
A Sanderson & Sons Ltd for the
refurbishment of Gawthorpe Hall.

J20   Artichoke   1895
Colour print from woodblocks
711 × 513 mm
Whitworth Art Gallery, University of
Manchester

J21   Fig and Peacock   1895
Colour print from woodblocks
900 × 543 mm
Whitworth Art Gallery, University of
Manchester

Fig and Peacock required twenty blocks
and was issued with a complementary
frieze. The Cabinet Maker and Art Furnisher
(December 1896 p146) described the

J14

block-printed version as 'most subdued
and full of repose', whilst the lacquered
and gilded example 'glowed with
lustrous effect'.

J22   Meadow Flowers   1896
Colour print from woodblocks
979 × 545 mm
Whitworth Art Gallery, University of
Manchester

The critic for *The Studio* thought that *Meadow
Flowers*, with its frieze *The May Tree* was
'perhaps amongst the most important' of
Crane's exhibits at the Arts and Crafts
Exhibition of 1896 and described the
combination as 'at once novel and
excellent'.

J23   The May Tree   1896
Colour print from woodblocks
527 × 889 mm
Whitworth Art Gallery, University of
Manchester
(ill p65)

A frieze for use with the *Meadow Flowers*
filling.

J24   Day Lily   1897
Colour print from woodblocks
790 × 545 mm
Whitworth Art Gallery, University of
Manchester
(ill p41)

J25   The National   1897
Colour print from woodblocks
750 × 510 mm
Whitworth Art Gallery, University of
Manchester

Designed to commemorate Queen
Victoria's Jubilee. Crane explained that
the general idea of the design was 'to
symbolise the unity of the kingdom,
while emphasising the National Emblems
and characteristics of the three countries
of which it is composed' (contemporary
advertisement).

J16

J26 Cockatoo and Pomegranate
1899
Colour print from woodblocks
876 × 508 mm
Whitworth Art Gallery, University of
Manchester
(ill p64)

shown with:
(i) Photograph of the Jeffrey & Co stand
at the Paris Exhibition, 1900 (courtesy of
The Board of Trustees of the Victoria and
Albert Museum)

(ii) Photograph of the design being
printed at Jeffrey & Co's Works, c1900
Leeds City Art Galleries

J27 Orange Tree 1902
Colour print from woodblocks
1568 × 1060 mm
Whitworth Art Gallery, University of
Manchester
(plate VI)

shown with:
(i) Four pear-wood printing blocks
A Sanderson & Sons Ltd

(ii) Three photographs illustrating the
hand-printing process (courtesy
A Sanderson & Sons Ltd)
(ill p62)

A wallpaper filling for use with the *Fruit*
frieze.

J28 Fruit 1903
Colour print from woodblocks
546 × 1010 mm
Whitworth Art Gallery, University of
Manchester

A wallpaper frieze for use with the *Orange
Tree* filling.

J29 Dulce Domum 1904
Colour print from woodblocks
965 × 510 mm
Whitworth Art Gallery, University of
Manchester

This was one of Crane's largest design
repeats.

J25

J30 Macaw 1908
Colour print from woodblocks
965 × 510 mm
A Sanderson & Sons Ltd

Designed specially for display at the
Franco-British Exhibition 1908, the *Macaw*
was described as a 'pièce de résistance'
(*Queen* 1909 p106).

J31 Two Wallpaper Log Books, Jeffrey & Co
(i) 1885-1900
(ii) 1902-1928
Showing production details of Crane's
designs, including *Woodnotes* and *Deer and
Rabbits* frieze.
A Sanderson & Sons Ltd

CHRISTINE WOODS

K Ceramics

Crane designed only a few ceramics, although they date from throughout his career. The examples gathered here were produced by three companies. Crane also worked for a fourth, Minton's, and his work was widely pirated by companies eager to cash in on his success as a children's book illustrator. Crane did not work for the mass market; his designs were hand-painted and expensive and they were often produced as 'one-offs' for prestigious displays at international exhibitions.

Josiah Wedgwood and Sons

Crane was introduced to the company by Mr and Mrs Wilbraham of Rode Hall, in 1866. He was sent a number of creamware vases which he painted in his studio and then returned to the factory for firing. The subjects Crane chose included *The Seasons*, *The Ages of Man*, *Painting*, and *Music*. A number of the pieces were shown at the Paris Exhibition of 1867 but none was produced commercially.

K1   Knowledge   1867
Creamware vase, hand-painted by Crane
Manufactured by Wedgwood
Height 242 mm
Inscribed: *Knowledge*; signed with monogram; impressed: *WEDGWOOD WUQ I*
The Wedgwood Museum, Stoke-on-Trent

K2   Imagination   1867
Creamware vase, hand-painted by Crane
Manufactured by Wedgwood
Height 242 mm
Inscribed: *Imagination*; signed with monogram; impressed: *WEDGWOOD WUQ I*
The Wedgwood Museum, Stoke-on-Trent

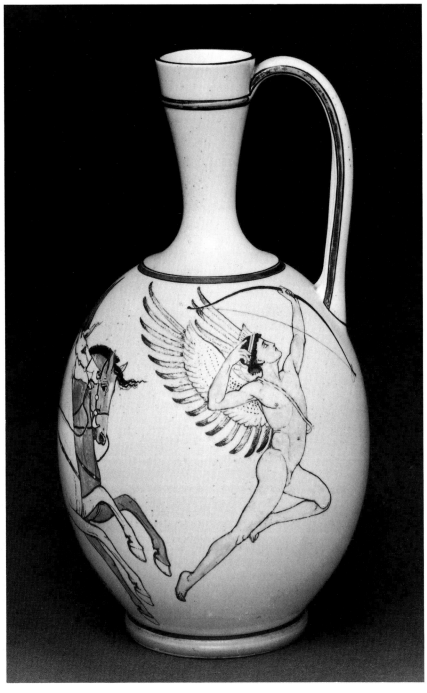

K2

In a letter to the company Crane said that he had 'endeavoured to represent – on the one – "Imagination" in her car drawn by winged horses ("Sight" & "Hearing") & the winged figure in front is "Thought". On the other vase – "Knowledge" in her car, with a figure ("Experience") guiding five horses (the "Senses") and Reason goes first with a torch' (Maureen Batkin, *Wedgwood Ceramics* 1982 p68).

K3 The Employments of Man 1867
Creamware vase, hand-painted by Crane
Manufactured by Wedgwood
Height 140 mm
Impressed: *WEDGWOOD WU S*
The Wedgwood Museum, Stoke-on-Trent

Maw & Co

K4 Nursery Rhymes c1875
Four encaustic tiles, hand-coloured over printed outline
Manufactured by Maw & Co
Each 155 mm square (6 in)
Inscribed on tiles: *Tom Tucker, Little Brown Betty, Jock he was a Piper's Son, Little Bo Peep*
Peter Rose and Albert Gallichan

Four from a series of eight (?) tiles; the missing scenes include *Mistress Mary,* and *Little Boy Blue.* As the advertisement of c1876 shows (K6i) the scenes were also produced as roundels. Crane thought 'that the square form, size, and treatment of the six-inch tiles suggested the adoption of the same size and treatment for 'The Baby's Opera' 1877 (A22); indeed the figures of *Little Bo Peep* and *Mistress Mary* were repeated in the book.

K5 The Seasons 1875
Four encaustic tiles, hand-coloured over printed outline
Manufactured by Maw & Co
Each 203 mm square (8 in)
Signed with monogram; one is dated 1875 on one edge
Inscribed on tiles: *Hiems, Ver, Aestas, Autumnus*
Peter Rose and Albert Gallichan

K8i

The designs are some of the most strictly classical that Crane produced. Restricted to simple outline and flat colour by the nature of the medium he turned to classical vase painting for inspiration.

K6 The Times of Day 1875
Four encaustic tiles, hand-coloured over printed outline
Manufactured by Maw & Co
Each 203 mm square (8 in)
Signed with monogram; one is dated 1875 on one edge; inscribed *Aurora, Meridies, Vesper, Nox*
Exh: Paris Exhibition, 1878
Peter Rose and Albert Gallichan
(ill p17)

shown with:
(i) *Advertisement for Tiles Manufactured by Maw and Co* c1876
Hornby Library, Liverpool City Libraries

Like K5 the slight repeat in the design suggests that they were intended to be hung vertically and were thus suited for a fireplace jamb. *Nox (Night)* is accompanied by the poppy, the plant of sleep.

K7 Ploughing 1889
Lustre tile panel (16 tiles), hand-painted
Manufactured by Maw & Co
345 × 1260 mm (each tile 150 mm square)
Signed with monogram
Exh: Paris Exhibition, 1889; A & C, 1889
The Board of Trustees of the Victoria and Albert Museum, London

Ploughing formed the lower frieze of a large tile panel on the theme of Labour designed by Crane and Lewis F Day. The two horizontal panels by Crane, *Ploughing, Sowing* and *Reaping* and an upright panel showing the *Triumph of Labour*, were framed by floral tiles by Day.

K8 Five Vases c1888–9
(i) *Swan*
Height 232 mm
(ill previous page)

(ii) *Ship*
Height 320 mm

(iii) *Divers*
Height 210 mm

K9

(iv) *Skoal*
Height 212 mm

(v) *Dancing Figures*
Height 305 mm
(ill p141)

Earthenware painted in ruby lustre on a cream ground
Manufactured by Maw & Co
Signed with monogram on the base
(i-iv) Richard Dennis
(v) Whitworth Art Gallery, University of Manchester

shown with:
(vi) *Three Sheets of Designs of Shapes for Vases for Maw and Co*
Pen and ink
Anthony Crane

Maw & Co's move into the field of Art Pottery gave Crane the opportunity of experimenting with different shapes as well as working for the first time with the new lustre glazes. The *Swan* vase (K8i) is the most striking example in the group of the unity of shape and decoration. It is in the form of a ship with the prow formed from the head of a swan and the stern from a fish's tail. Aside from the range of shapes produced, another feature of interest is the range of effects which Crane is able to achieve using a single colour against a plain ground.

Pilkington's Tile and Pottery Company

This company was formed in 1891 with William Burton, formerly a chemist at Wedgwood's, as the manager. Joined by his brother Joseph in 1895 they began a

long series of experiments leading to a
wide range of rich glazes which became
the hallmark of the company. In the initial
period, however, they concentrated on
the production of tiles and it was in this
capacity that Crane was first employed.
His introduction probably came through
Lewis F Day, a friend who, as a salaried
employee, had a great influence on their
artistic output. At the Paris Exhibition of
1900 the company showed designs by
Voysey, Day, Frederic Shields as well as
Crane's large five-panel series of *The Senses*.

In 1903 William Burton decided to
diversify into decorative glazed pottery
which he named Lancastrian Pottery.
Influenced by Lewis F Day, Burton's
ideas on pottery echoed those of Crane
himself; he wished to use 'shapes, based
on either the forms of the Greek, Persian
or Chinese pottery, on some suggestions
of natural growth, or on the forms
actually evolved from plastic clay in the
hands of the potter' (*Lancastrian Pottery*
1986 p3). Another feature of the company's philosophy which appealed to
Crane was the freedom of interpretation
given to the painters. Burton gathered a
talented team together which included
William Mycock, Charles Cundall and
Richard Joyce, all of whom have signed
works in this exhibition.

K9   Flora's Retinue   c1900-1

Six earthenware tiles with designs
impressed in raised outline and painted
Manufactured by Pilkington's
Each 151 mm square (6 in)
Mark: a raised P
Exh: Glasgow Exhibition, 1901
The Board of Trustees of the Victoria and
Albert Museum, London
(ill previous page)

The designs, showing *Poppy*, *Bluebell*,
Daffodil, *Cornflower*, *Columbine* and *Anemone*,
show floral personifications similar to
those in gift books such as *Flora's Feast*
1889 (A34).

K10   Peacock   1906

Lustre dish, painted by Charles Cundall
Manufactured by Pilkington's
Diameter 482 mm

K11

Marks: *PL* in monogram, *ENGLAND, VI,*
2477 all impressed; *WC, CEC* both in
monogram in lustre
The Board of Trustees of the Victoria and
Albert Museum, London

K11   Peacock

Lustre plaque, painted anonymously
Manufactured by Pilkington's
Diameter 241 mm
Signed with monogram on the face
Peter Rose and Albert Gallichan

Crane's use of the Peacock motif cuts
across his work, appearing in wallpapers,
book illustrations, paintings and
drawings. Here the motif is sanctioned
by the circular format which it fills very
effectively. The dish and the plaque are
similar except for the border on the plate
which seems to have been added by the
painter who worked with some licence
from Crane's drawing.

K12   St George   1906

Lustre plaque, painted by Richard Joyce
Manufactured by Pilkington's
Diameter 290 mm
Signed with monogram on the face;
inscribed on the border *Un Chevalier Sans*
Peur Et Sans Reproche; marks on the reverse:
PL in monogram, *VI, ENGLAND* all
impressed; *RJ* in monogram in lustre
Whitworth Art Gallery, University of
Manchester

The inscription *A Knight Without Fear And*
Reproach refers to le Chevalier de Bayard, a
French knight of the time of Francis I,
although the image shows St George and
the dragon.

K13   Dancing Figures with Lilies and Fruiting Trees   1906

Lustre vase, painted by Richard Joyce
Manufactured by Pilkington's

UN CHEVALIER SANS PEUR ET SANS REPROCHE

K12

Height 330 mm
Signed with monogram; inscribed RJ,
1906
Richard Dennis

K14 Bon Accorde 1907
Lustre vase, painted by Richard Joyce
Manufactured by Pilkington's
Height 225 mm
Inscribed: 2475, *PL* in monogram, *VII*,
ENGLAND all impressed; Crane's mono-
gram, *DES, RJ, PINX. 1907* in lustre
Manchester City Art Galleries
(plate VIII)

K15 Dancing Figures (Liberty)
1910
Lustre vase, painted by Richard Joyce
Manufactured by Pilkington's
Height 267 mm

Inscribed: 2671, *PL* in monogram, *IX*,
ENGLAND all impressed; Crane's monogram, *DES, RJ, PINX. 1910* in lustre
Manchester City Art Galleries
(ill next page)

The design is related to a vase (K8v)
designed for Maw & Co, and a textile, *The
British Empire 1887*, for Edmund Potter &
Co (H1). The vase is found in two
versions; in one, as here, the dancers

wear the cap of Liberty and hold up lamps
linked with chains and in the other they
hold up garlands of flowers.

K16 Lion 1911
Lustre bowl, painted by Charles Cundall
Manufactured by Pilkington's
Height 123 mm
Inscribed: 2469, *PL* in monogram, *XI*,
ENGLAND all impressed; Crane's
monogram, *DES, CEC, PINX. 1911*
in lustre
Manchester City Art Galleries

K17 The Swan Ship 1912
Lustre vase, painted by William Mycock
Manufactured by Pilkington's
Height 254 mm
Inscribed: 2472, *PL* in monogram, *X*,
ENGLAND all impressed; *WSM* in
monogram in lustre; *X. 1912* incised
Manchester City Art Galleries

This, the most popular of Crane's designs,
exists in a number of different colour
variations executed by several painters.
The design is closer to a tile designed for
Maw & Co, *Luna*, than the eccentric vase
of the same name (K8i) and is similar to
the printed silk *The Four Seasons* 1893 (H5).

K18 Rhine Maidens
Vase, moulded with a blue glaze
Manufactured by Pilkington's
Height 92 mm
Signed with monogram on the body; bee
mark on the base
Peter Rose and Albert Gallichan

GREG SMITH

K15

L   Stained Glass

In spite of designing stained glass only sporadically Crane had much to say on the subject. He strongly advocated the proper use of the lead lines which he thought 'ought to be fairly complete and agreeable as an arrangement of line even without the colour' (Crane, *Art Journal* p20). On the subject of colour Crane saw the danger of the use of white since it lead to 'holes in the window' and called instead for the bold use of colour to create what he called a 'network of jewelled light', a 'translucent mosaic' (Crane, *Bases* pp137–54).

L1   Cartoon for Stained Glass: 'Sphaera Imaginationis'   c1889

Pencil, pen and watercolour
113 × 609 mm
Signed: *WALTER CRANE DEL: ET INV*
Exh: A & C, 1889 (95)
William Morris Gallery, Walthamstow

This cartoon is for one of two stained-glass panels which Crane designed for the doors of the picture gallery of Sir Aston Webb's home, Clare Lawn (ill p52). The two figures symbolise the twin sources of artistic inspiration – Nature and the Imagination. The panels were made by Morris & Co and painted by Bowman and Dearle and show Crane's sparer approach to glass for a domestic interior.

L2   Six Designs for the Church of the Agapemone, Stamford Hill, London

1895
(i) *Moon and Stars*
(ii) *Olive Trees*
(iii) *Irises*
(iv) *Corn and Poppy*
(v) *White Lily*
(vi) *Death and Night* (ill p149)
Watercolour and gouache
All 518 × 342 mm (1½in scale)
Royal Borough of Kensington and Chelsea Library and Arts Service

L1

It was not until the 1890s and his collaboration with James Silvester Sparrow that Crane made a distinctive contribution to stained glass. The most important of their projects was the design and execution of a set of windows for the Church of the Agapemone, the Ark of the Covenant, Stamford Hill. The church was designed by Joseph Morris & Co and it was they who, on behalf of the Building Committee, wrote to Crane inviting him to submit designs. The Committee had chosen two texts: the *Benedicite* and *Psalm 148*, and the letter sent to Crane in May 1895 included a plan of the church with suggested subjects. At some stage he changed the brief so that the two-light aisle windows were filled with floral designs including the rose, lily, vine, olive, fig and iris. Some of these have a clear religious significance but others have more in common with the decorative floral vocabulary which he had developed during the 1880s. The meaning of the main windows is also not without interest: the large four-light west window showing the *Sun of Righteousness* was juxtaposed with smaller lights showing *Sin and Death* and *Death and Disease* which are understood to be driven away by the light of the new day.

The extraordinarily rich effect produced by the glass had much to do with the techniques and materials used by Sparrow. In *The Bases of Design* Crane gave a detailed account of their working methods, from the coloured $1\frac{1}{2}$ in scale drawing through to the full-scale cartoons with the lead lines marked, to the choice of glass (much of which was manufactured by Messrs Briton & Gibson), and the various finishing touches. Crane talks of the principle of 'variety in unity' the effect arising 'not in the juxtaposition of dark and light pieces of one colour merely, but by the bold arrangement of various colours, having the effect of one, but with a richness and sonorousness that the single tint does not possess' (Crane, *Bases* p 150).

The Ark of the Covenant.

Elevation of small western Window.

When looking at the Central or Rising Sun Window this window would be seen on the Spectators right.

L2vi

L3 Design for a Stained-Glass Window: St Cecilia 1898
Watercolour and gouache
Signed and dated: *Walter Crane. May/1898*;
inscribed: *SKETCH. DESIGN. 1½ SCALE. FOR. WINDOW. IN. TER. AA. Ch*
572 × 194 mm
Guildhall Art Gallery, London

GREG SMITH

Opposite
Walter Crane 'Sin and Death' from the Church of the Agapemone, Stamford
Hill 1895, stained glass

List of Lenders

Belfast, Ulster Museum : C28
Birmingham, Museum and Art Gallery : D2i-ii
Bristol, Art Gallery : B9
Cambridge, Fitzwilliam Museum : A24i, A41i-ix, C14
Anthony Crane : A3i-iii, A9, A12i, A16i-ii, A19i-vi, A22v,
    A23ix, A25i-iii, A26i-iii, B10ii-iii, B16, B18, B20-21, B26,
    C1i-v, C2i-v, C3-4i-iv, C7, C9-13, C15-16, C21i-viii, C22i-v,
    C23i-ix, C33i-ii, C34, C37, D1i-ii, D5i-ii, D6i-ii, F2ii, H4ii-
    iii, H11, H13i-vii, J13i
Glasgow, Art Gallery and Museum : A17i-vii, A40vii, B4
Leeds, City Art Galleries : D3, J3, J26ii
Liverpool, Hornby Library (Liverpool City Libraries) : A6, A8,
    A11-14, A16-20, A22-24, A29, A38, A42ii-iii, B13i-iii, B15,
    B23, B24i-ii, K6i
Liverpool, Walker Art Gallery (National Museums on
    Merseyside) : B1, B5, C29
London, Art Workers' Guild : E2vi
London, The Trustees of The British Museum : A22i-iv, A23i-
    viii, A40i-vi, C31
London, EETPU : B10i
London, Guildhall Art Gallery : L3
London, Labour Party Archives : B3, B6-7, B14
London, Royal Borough of Kensington and Chelsea Library and
    Arts Service : B12, B22, C5-6, C35-37i-iii, E2iv-v, F1i-vii,
    F2i,iii-v, F4, G1-2, G4i-iv, G5i-v, H10i, J8i, J13ii-vi, J17i,
    L2i-vi
London, A Sanderson & Sons Ltd : J1i, J19i, J27i-ii, J30, J31i-ii
London, The Trustees of The Tate Gallery : D4
London, The Board of Trustees of the Victoria and Albert
    Museum : B11i-ii, C27, E2ii-iii, F3, H1, H6i, H9, H12, J1-2,
    J4-5, J26i, K7, K9-10
London, William Morris Gallery : B8, D1, D7, E2i, L1
Manchester, Central Reference Library : A1i-iv, A27
Manchester, City Art Galleries : A5i-iii, E1, J11, K14-17
Manchester, Polytechnic Library : A4, A15, A28, A30, A31i-ii,
    A32-33, A36, A39, A41, A42i, B2, B19i-v, B21i, B22i, J12
Manchester University, John Rylands Library : A2, A21i-ii, A35,
    A37, A40
Manchester University, Whitworth Art Gallery : A34, B17, C17,
    C19, C30, G3, H2-3, H4i, H5, H7-8, H10, J1iii, J6, J8-10,
    J13-17, J19-29, K8v, K12
National Trust : J18
New York, The FORBES Magazine Collection : C26, C32
Oxford, The Visitors of the Ashmolean Museum : C8
Private Collections : B25, C18, C20, C24-25, D8, H14, J7, K4-6,
    K8i-iv, K11, K13, K18
Stoke-on-Trent, The Wedgwood Museum : K1-3

Photographic Acknowledgements

We would like to thank lenders to the exhibition for permission
to reproduce items in the catalogue. We also acknowledge the
following :

Bodleian Library, Oxford : p71
Fitzwilliam Museum, Cambridge : p142
Martin Harrison : p149
Historical Monuments Commission : p56
Hornby Library, Liverpool City Libraries : pp33, 35, 49, 72
National Art Library, London : p48
National Museums on Merseyside, Walker Art Gallery : p18
National Portrait Gallery, London : pp12, 106
Neue Pinakothek, Munich : p19
Rothschild Collections Ltd : p16
Royal Borough of Kensington and Chelsea Library and Arts
    Service : pp50, 52, 53
A Sanderson & Sons Ltd : p62
Trustees of the Victoria and Albert Museum, London : p60
Whitworth Art Gallery, University of Manchester : pp39, 64
William Morris Gallery, Walthamstow : p18